Teacher Resource Key Stage

PHONICS ACTIVITIES 1

Initial Consonants and Short Vowels

BRIGHTER™ VISION

Brighter Vision Education Ltd.,
Eton House, 18-24 Paradise Road, Richmond, Surrey TW9 1SR

Copyright 1996 Brighter Vision Education Ltd.

™ is a trademark of Brighter Vision Education Ltd.

Some material used in this book is used under licence from
Frank Schaffer Publications Inc.

All rights reserved. This book is sold subject to the condition that it shall not, by way of trade or otherwise, be lent, hired out or otherwise circulated without the publisher's prior consent in any form of binding or cover other than that in which it is published and without a similar condition, including this condition, being imposed upon the subsequent purchaser.

No part of this publication may be reproduced, stored in a retrieval system, or transmitted, in any form or by any means, electronic, mechanical, photocopying, recording or otherwise, without the prior written permission of the publisher, except where expressly permitted. This book remains copyright, although permission is granted to copy pages 1 to 99 for classroom distribution and use only in the school which has purchased the book.

Consultant Editor: Pam Hutchinson

Printed in Belgium
Reprinted 1998

BV-05-301 Teacher Resource Key Stage 1/P1-P3: Phonics Activities 1
ISBN 1 86172 022 X

INTRODUCTION

This set of 98 phonics activity sheets has been designed to support and consolidate the development of your pupils' listening, reading and writing skills.

To enable you to select appropriate material for your class and for individual pupils, the activities are grouped as follows:

★ initial consonants
★ initial and final consonants
★ short vowel a
★ short vowel e
★ short vowel i
★ short vowel o
★ short vowel u
★ review of short vowels

The detailed contents list gives a short description of each activity and there is sufficient reinforcement of each consonant and short vowel to ensure that, however much practice pupils may need, it will be varied and enjoyable.

Give your pupils the firm foundation they need by using selected, appropriate activities from the book. Once they are confident in their consonant and short vowel knowledge, move on to consonant blends and long and special vowels. These are covered in Phonics Activities 2, another volume in this series.

CONTENTS

Initial Consonants
b — Letters and pictures 1
c — Letters and pictures..........2
d — Letters and pictures 3
f — Letters and pictures 4
g — Letters and pictures..........5
h — Letters and pictures 6
j — Letters and pictures 7
k — Letters and pictures 8
l — Letters and pictures 9
m — Letters and pictures 10
n — Letters and pictures 11
p — Letters and pictures 12
q — Letters and pictures 13
r — Letters and pictures 14
s — Letters and pictures 15
t — Letters and pictures 16
v — Letters and pictures 17
w — Letters and pictures 18
y — Letters and pictures 19
z — Letters and pictures 20

Initial and Final Consonants
Missing letters 21
Consonant crossword 22

Short Vowel a
ad — Rhyming words 23
ad — Writing words................24
ad — Finding words................25
ad — Unscrambling words 26
at — Rhyming words 27
at — Writing words................28
at — Unscrambling words 29
at — Finding words 30
an — Rhyming words 31
an — Writing words................32
an — Finding words 33
an — Unscrambling words 34

Short Vowel e
en — Rhyming words.............35
en — Writing words................36
en — Finding words 37
en — Unscrambling words 38
ed — Rhyming words 39
ed — Writing words................40
ed — Finding words 41
ed — Unscrambling words 42
et — Rhyming words 43
et — Writing words 44
et — Finding words 45
et — Unscrambling words 46

Short Vowel i
it — Rhyming words................47
it — Writing words 48
it — Finding words..................49
it — Unscrambling words........50
ig — Rhyming words 51
ig — Writing words.................52
ig — Finding words 53
ig — Unscrambling words 54
ip — Rhyming words 55
ip — Writing words 56
ip — Finding words 57
ip — Unscrambling words 58

IV

CONTENTS

Short Vowel o
   og — Rhyming words 59
   og — Writing words 60
   og — Finding words 61
   og — Unscrambling words 62
   op — Rhyming words 63
   op — Writing words 64
   op — Finding words 65
   op — Unscrambling words 66
   ot — Rhyming words 67
   ot — Writing words 68
   ot — Finding words 69
   ot — Unscrambling words 70

Short Vowel u
   ub — Rhyming words 71
   ub — Writing words 72
   ub — Finding words 73
   ub — Unscrambling words 74
   un — Rhyming words 75
   un — Writing words 76
   un — Finding words 77
   un — Unscrambling words 78
   ug — Rhyming words 79
   ug — Writing words 80
   ug — Finding words 81
   ug — Unscrambling words 82

Short Vowel Review
   a, i — Missing vowels 83
   a, i — Matching 84
   a, i — Sentence completion 85
   a, i — Sentence completion 86
   i, o — Sentence completion 87
   a, u — Sentence completion 88

   o, u — Sentence completion 89
   a, i, o — Missing letters 90
   e, o, u — Missing letters 91
   a, i, o, u — Missing letters 92
   a, i, o, u — Writing vowels 93
   a, e, i, o, u — Matching 94
   a, e, i, o, u — Missing vowels 95
   a, e, i, o, u — Matching 96
   a, e, i, o, u — Matching 97
   a, e, i, o, u — Matching 98

Answer key
   99-123

Name _____ Initial consonant **b**

Say the name of each picture. Write the beginning letter.

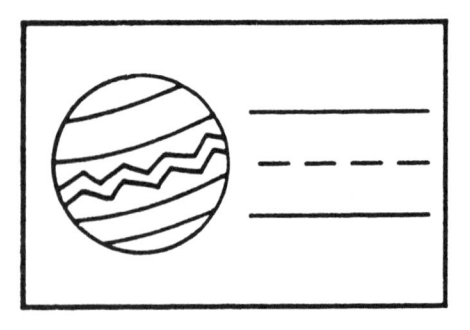

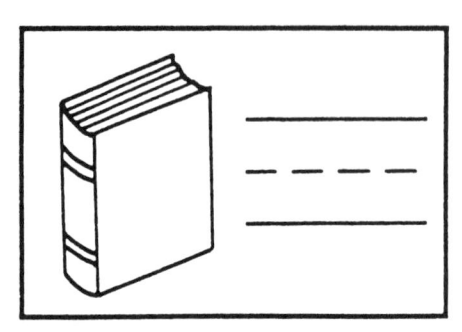

Colour the pictures that begin with **b**.

Brainwork! Draw six pictures that begin with **b**.

1

Copyright © 1996 Brighter Vision Education Ltd   Phonics, KS1

Name _____ Initial consonant c

Say the name of each picture. Write the beginning letter.

Colour the pictures that begin with **c**.

Brainwork! Draw six pictures that begin with **c**.

2

Copyright © 1996 Brighter Vision Education Ltd   Phonics, KS1

Name _____ Initial consonant **d**

Say the name of each picture. Write the beginning letter.

Colour the pictures that begin with **d**.

Brainwork! Draw six pictures that begin with **d**.

Name _____   Initial consonant **f**

Say the name of each picture. Write the beginning letter.

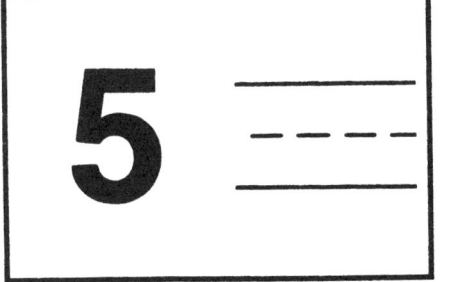

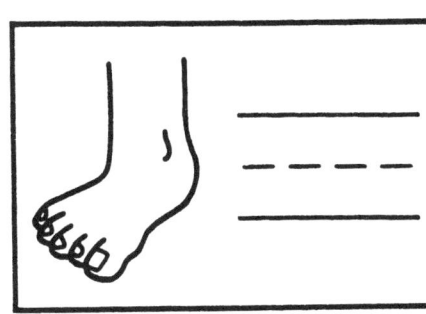

Colour the pictures that begin with **f**.

Brainwork! Draw six pictures that begin with **f**.

4

Copyright © 1996 Brighter Vision Education Ltd   Phonics, KS1

Name _____ Initial consonant **g**

Say the name of each picture. Write the beginning letter.

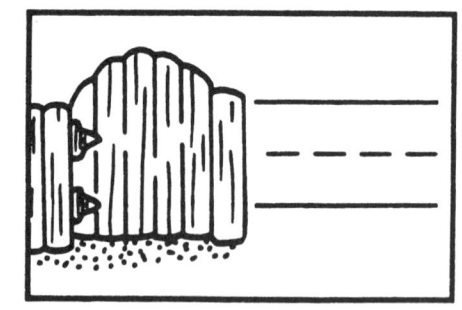

Colour the pictures that begin with **g**.

Brainwork! Draw six pictures that begin with **g**.

5

Copyright © 1996 Brighter Vision Education Ltd   Phonics, KS1

Name _____   Initial consonant **h**

Say the name of each picture. Write the beginning letter.

Colour the pictures that begin with **h**.

Brainwork! Draw six pictures that begin with **h**.

Copyright © 1996 Brighter Vision Education Ltd   Phonics, KS1

Name _____ Initial consonant **j**

Say the name of each picture. Write the beginning letter.

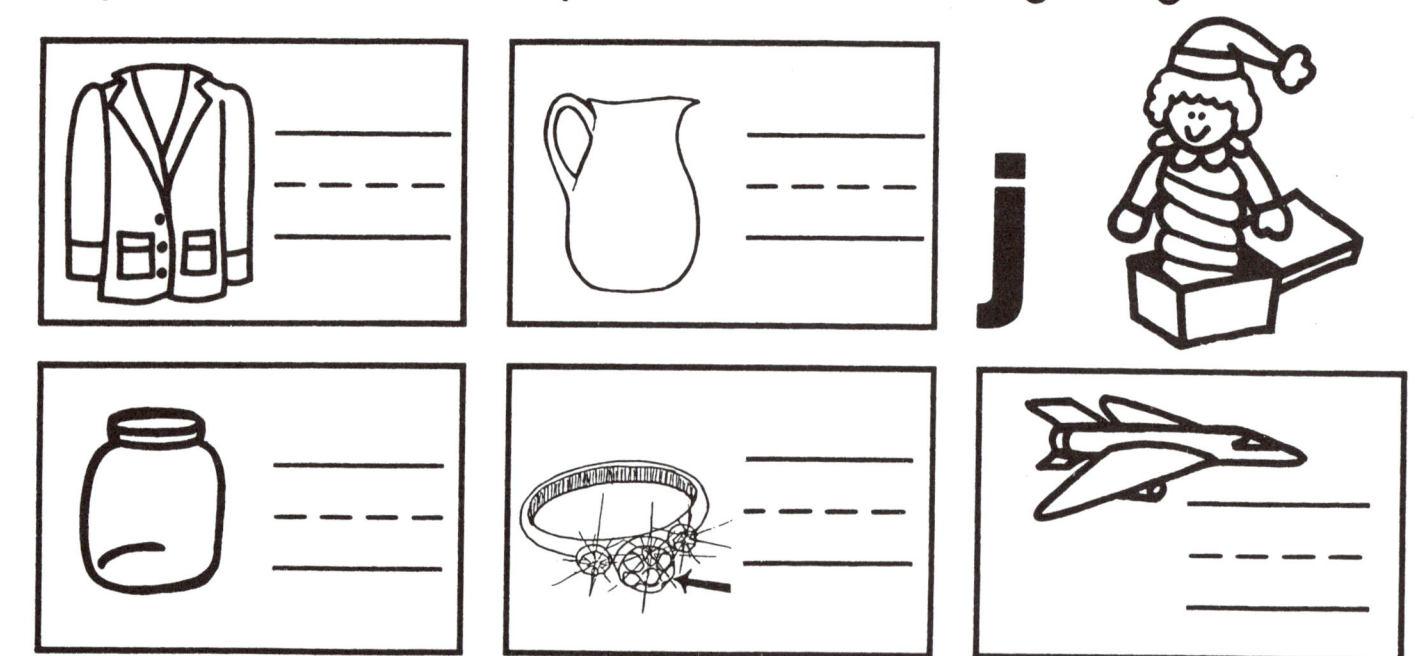

Colour the pictures that begin with **j**.

Brainwork! Draw six pictures that begin with **j**.

7

Copyright © 1996 Brighter Vision Education Ltd

Phonics, KS1

Name _____ Initial consonant **k**

Say the name of each picture. Write the beginning letter.

k

Colour the pictures that begin with **k**.

Brainwork! Draw six pictures that begin with **k**.

8

Copyright © 1996 Brighter Vision Education Ltd

Phonics, KS1

Name _____ Initial consonant l

Say the name of each picture. Write the beginning letter.

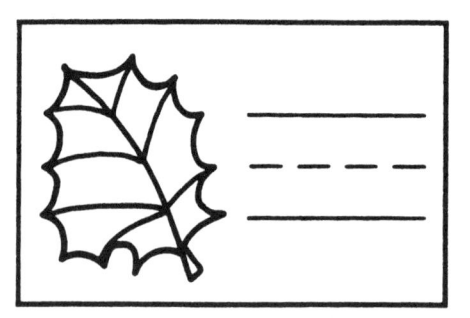

Colour the pictures that begin with l.

Brainwork! Draw six pictures that begin with l.

9

Name _____ Initial consonant **m**

Say the name of each picture. Write the beginning letter.

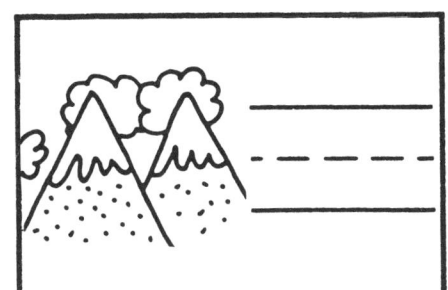

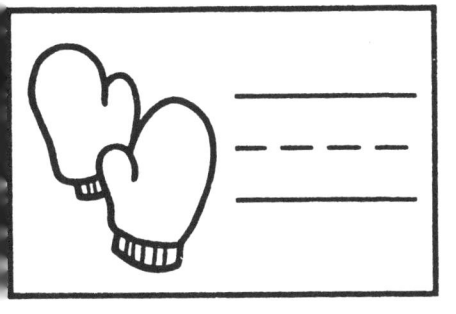

m

Colour the pictures that begin with **m**.

Brainwork! Draw six pictures that begin with **m**.

Name _____ Initial consonant **n**

Say the name of each picture. Write the beginning letter.

Colour the pictures that begin with **n**.

Brainwork! Draw six pictures that begin with **n**.

11

Copyright © 1996 Brighter Vision Education Ltd   Phonics, KS1

Name _____ Initial consonant **p**

Say the name of each picture. Write the beginning letter.

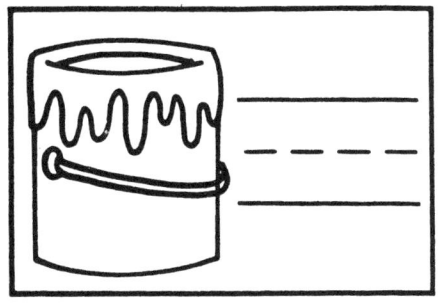

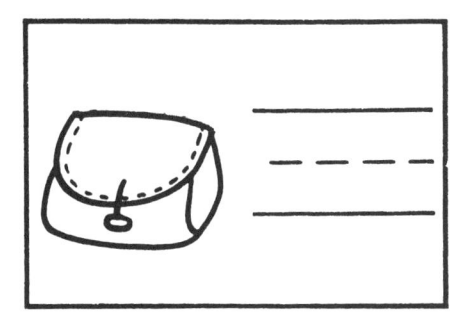

Colour the pictures that begin with **p**.

Brainwork! Draw six pictures that begin with **p**.

12

Copyright © 1996 Brighter Vision Education Ltd

Phonics, KS1

Name _____ Initial consonant q

Say the name of each picture. Write the beginning letter.

Colour the pictures that begin with **q**.

Brainwork! Draw six pictures that begin with **q**.

13

Name _____ Initial consonant **r**

Say the name of each picture. Write the beginning letter.

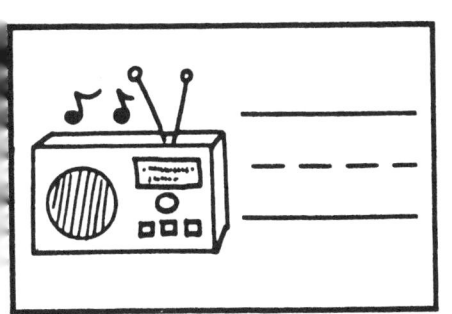

r

Colour the pictures that begin with **r**.

Brainwork! Draw six pictures that begin with **r**.

14

Name _____ Initial consonant **s**

Say the name of each picture. Write the beginning letter.

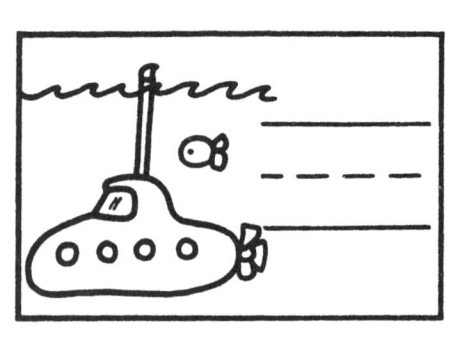

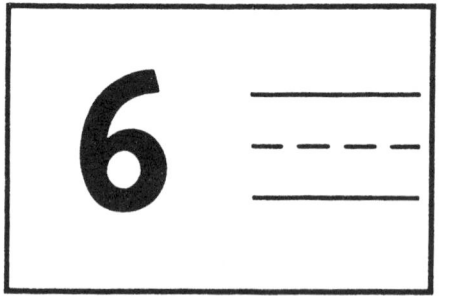

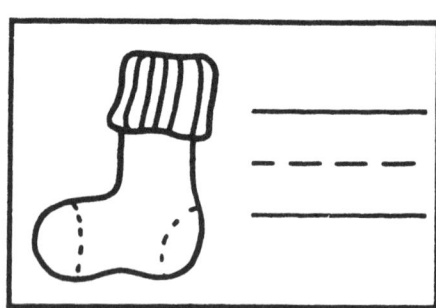

Colour the pictures that begin with **s**.

Brainwork! Draw six pictures that begin with **s**.

15

Copyright © 1996 Brighter Vision Education Ltd

Phonics, KS1

Name _____   Initial consonant t

Say the name of each picture. Write the beginning letter.

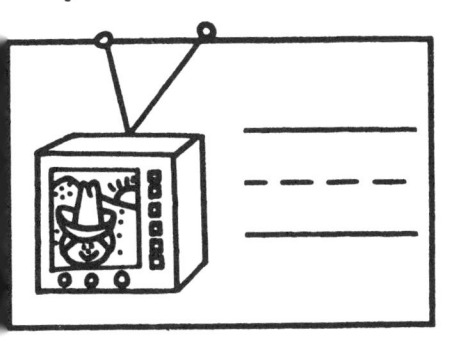

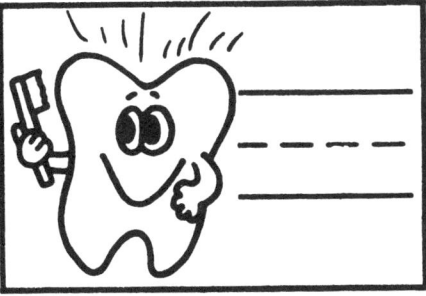

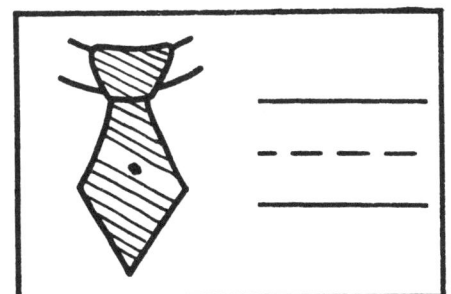

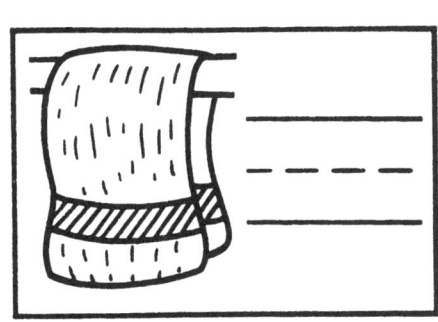

t

Colour the pictures that begin with **t**.

Brainwork! Draw six pictures that begin with **t**.

16

Copyright © 1996 Brighter Vision Education Ltd   Phonics, KS1

Name _____ Initial consonant **v**

Say the name of each picture. Write the beginning letter.

v

Colour the pictures that begin with **v**.

Brainwork! Draw six pictures that begin with **v**.

Name _____ Initial consonant **w**

Say the name of each picture. Write the beginning letter.

Colour the pictures that begin with **w.**

Brainwork! Draw six pictures that begin with **w.**

18

Copyright © 1996 Brighter Vision Education Ltd

Phonics, KS1

Name _____ Initial consonant y

Say the name of each picture. Write the beginning letter.

y

Colour the pictures that begin with y.

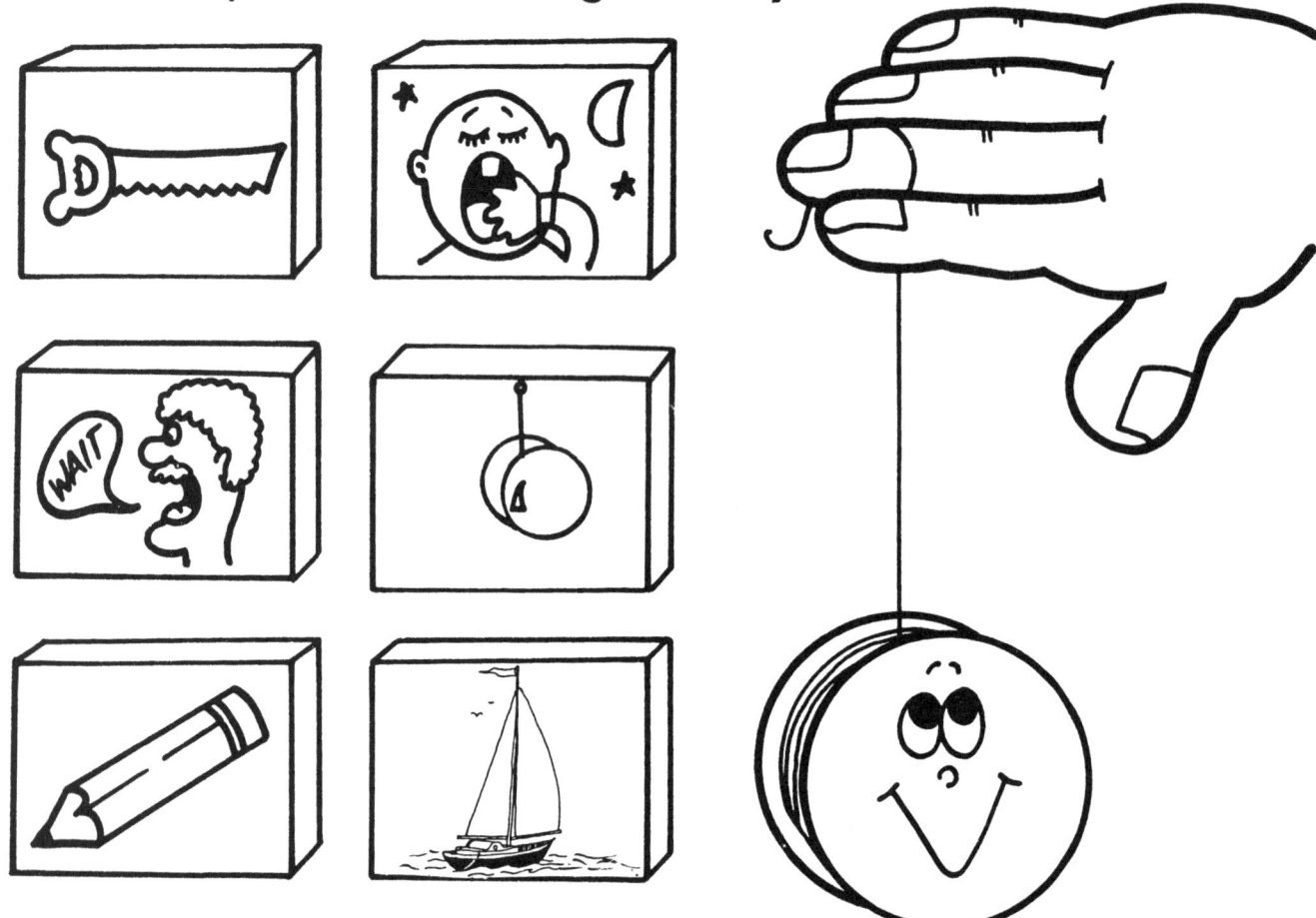

Brainwork! Draw six pictures that begin with y.

19

Copyright © 1996 Brighter Vision Education Ltd Phonics, KS1

Name _____ Initial consonant **z**

Say the name of each picture. Write the beginning letter.

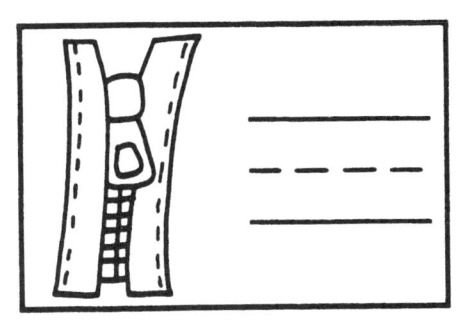

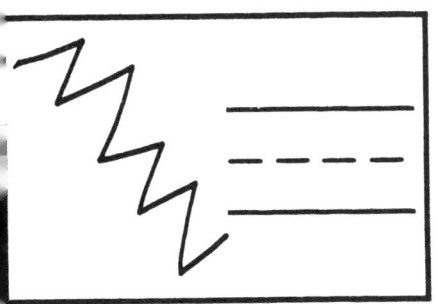

Colour the pictures that begin with **z**.

Brainwork! Draw six pictures that begin with **z**.

20

Name _____ Initial and final consonants

Print the beginning and ending letters.

_ a _	_ e _	_ u _
_ i _	_ o _	_ a _
_ o _	_ a _	_ e _
_ u _	_ i _	_ o _

21

Copyright © 1996 Brighter Vision Education Ltd   Phonics, KS1

Name _____   Initial and final consonants

Use the pictures to finish the puzzle.
The words go ↓ then →.

Name _____

-ad words

Help Otto Octopus make words.

1 _____
2 _____
3 _____
4 _____
5 _____
6 _____

Hi kids!

Colour the rhyming fish.

cab can dad lad pad bad sad mad rat

Phonics, KS1

Name _____ -ad words

Write each word three times.

| bad |
| dad |
| lad |
| sad |

24

Copyright © 1996 Brighter Vision Education Ltd　　　　　　　　　　　　　　　　　　　　Phonics, KS1

Name _____

-ad words

Find the words on Silly Sea Serpent. Write them on the lines below.

1 _____
2 _____
3 _____
4 _____
5 _____
6 _____

Start here

25

Copyright © 1996 Brighter Vision Education Ltd
Phonics, KS1

Name _____   -ad words

Unscramble the spelling words.

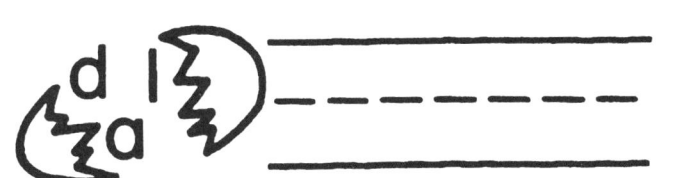

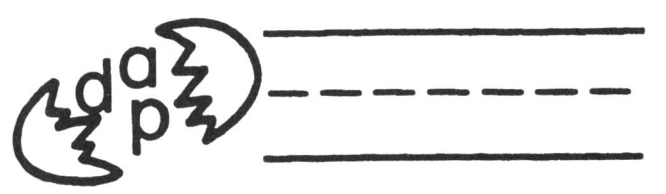

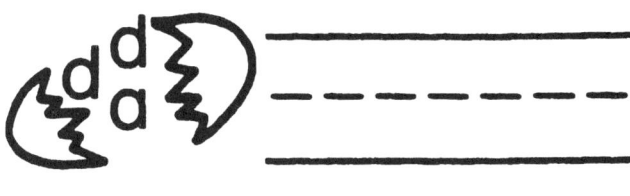

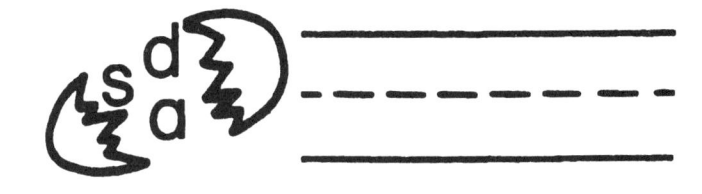

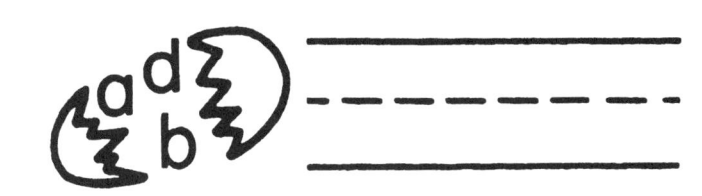

d l a _____

a d h _____

d a p _____

d d a _____

s d a _____

a d b _____

Now draw pictures of these words.

| dad | pad | lad |

26

Copyright © 1996 Brighter Vision Education Ltd   Phonics, KS1

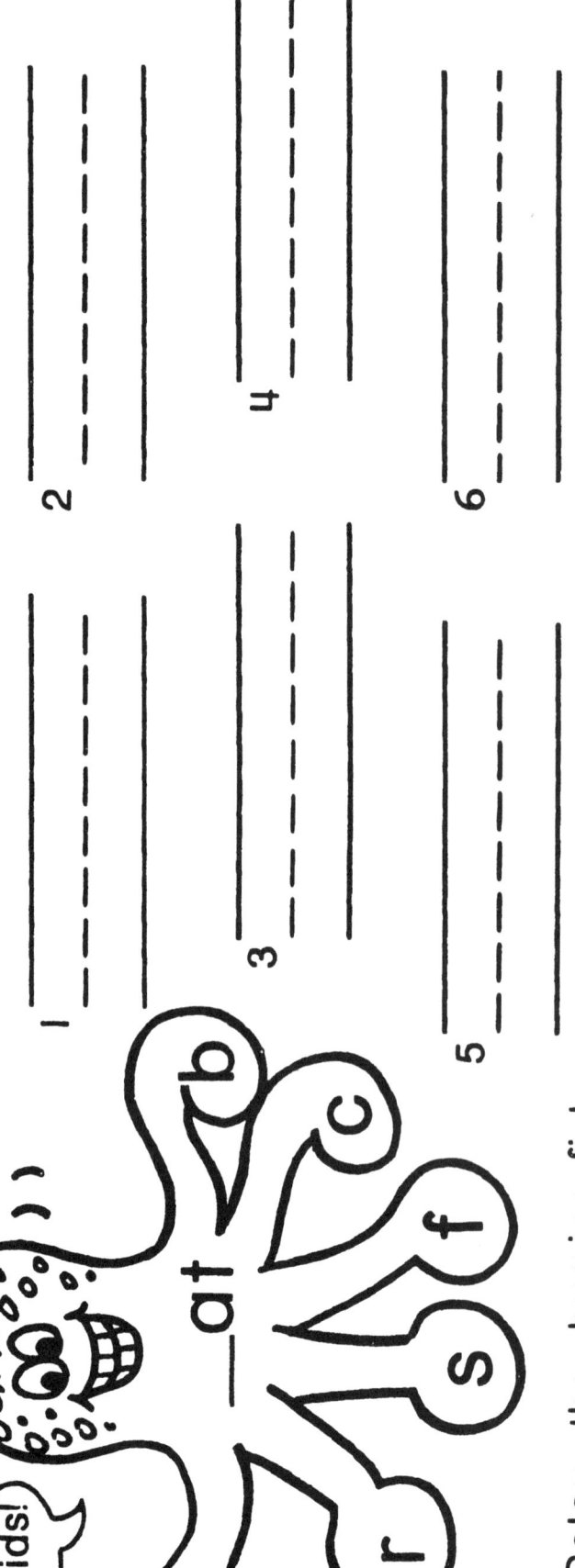

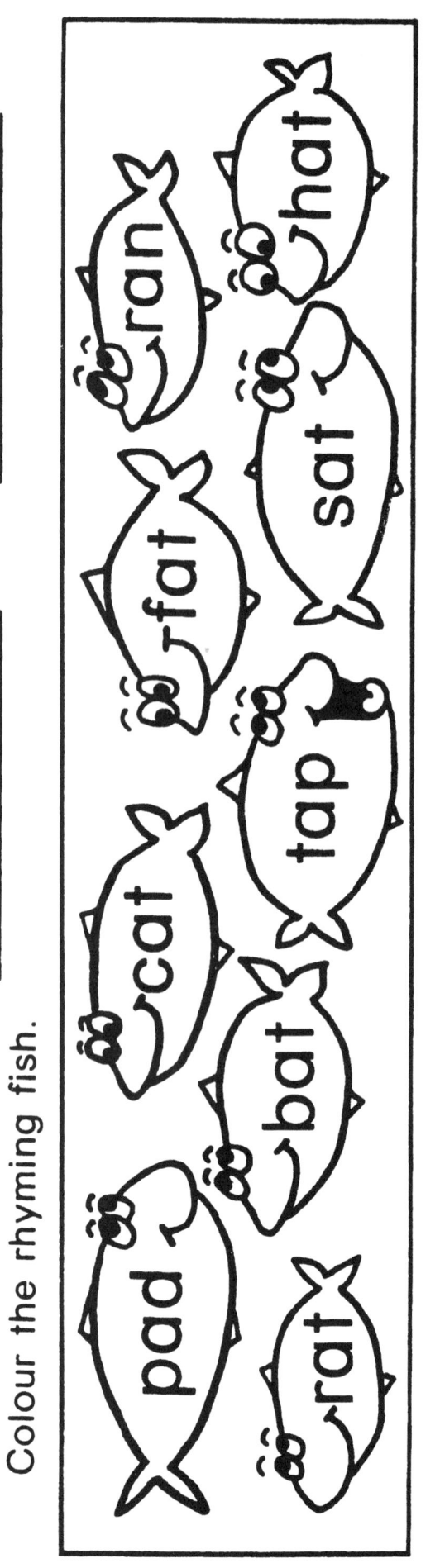

Name _____

-at words

Help Otto Octopus make words.

1 _____ 2 _____

3 _____ 4 _____

5 _____ 6 _____

Hi kids!

b c f s r h _at

Colour the rhyming fish.

ran hat fat sat tap cat bat pad rat

Copyright © 1996 Brighter Vision Education Ltd

Phonics, KS1

Name _____ -at words

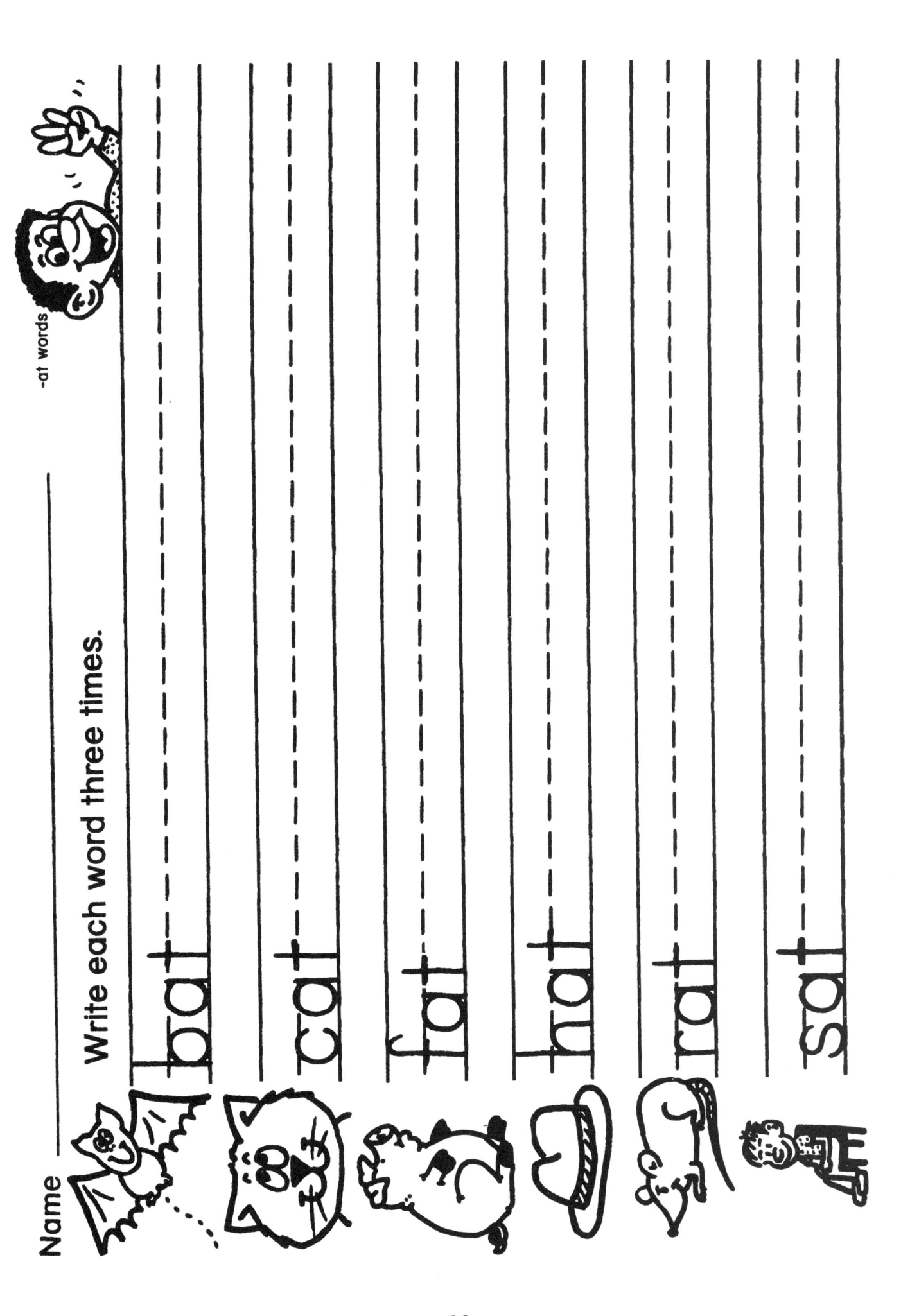

Write each word three times.

bat

cat

fat

hat

rat

sat

28

Copyright © 1996 Brighter Vision Education Ltd   Phonics, KS1

Name _____   -at words

Unscramble the words.

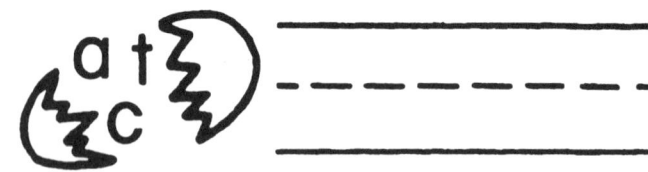

a s t _____

t f a _____

b t a _____

t a h _____

t r a _____

a t c _____

Now draw pictures of these words.

| hat | bat | rat |

29

Copyright © 1996 Brighter Vision Education Ltd   Phonics, KS1

Name _____ -at words

Find the words on Silly Sea Serpent. Write them on the lines below.

1 _____
2 _____
3 _____
4 _____
5 _____
6 _____

Start here →

f a t
a
c a t
s a t
r a t
h a t
b a t

30

Copyright © 1996 Brighter Vision Education Ltd   Phonics, KS1

Name _____

-an words

Help Otto Octopus make words.

1 _____   2 _____

3 _____   4 _____

5 _____   6 _____

"Hi kids!"

c   r   t   p   m   f   _an

Colour the rhyming fish.

sad   cap   ran   hat   man   fan   pan   can   tan

31

Copyright © 1996 Brighter Vision Education Ltd   Phonics, KS1

Name _____

-an words

Write each word three times.

can _____

fan _____

man _____

pan _____

ran _____

tan _____

32

Copyright © 1996 Brighter Vision Education Ltd

Phonics, KS1

Name _____ -an words

Find the words on Silly Sea Serpent. Write them on the lines below.

1 _____

2 _____

3 _____

4 _____

5 _____

6 _____

Name _____   -an words

Unscramble the words.

c n a _____

n f a _____

a n m _____

n a v _____

n r a _____

t a n _____

Now draw pictures of these words.

| fan | man | van |

Name _____ —en words

Help Otto Octopus make words.

1 _____
2 _____
3 _____
4 _____
5 _____
6 _____

"Hi kids!"

h, d, t, m, B, p — _en

Colour the rhyming fish.

Ben, ten, pen, den, then, web, jet, red, men

Name _____

―en words

Write each word three times.

Ben _____

hen _____

men _____

pen _____

ten _____

36

Copyright © 1996 Brighter Vision Education Ltd

Phonics, KS1

Name _____ —en words

Find the words on Silly Sea Serpent. Write them on the lines below.

1 _____
2 _____
3 _____
4 _____
5 _____
6 _____

Start here

37

Copyright © 1996 Brighter Vision Education Ltd   Phonics, KS1

Name _____   —en words

Unscramble the words.

n h e _____

e n p _____

e d n _____

n e B _____

n e k _____

n e m _____

Now draw pictures of these words.

| hen | pen | men |

38

Copyright © 1996 Brighter Vision Education Ltd   Phonics, KS1

Name _____

-ed words

Help Otto Octopus make words.

Hi kids!

b f w T l r _ed

1 _____
2 _____
3 _____
4 _____
5 _____
6 _____

Colour the rhyming fish.

net led bed peg wed red den Ted fed

39

Copyright © 1996 Brighter Vision Education Ltd

Phonics, KS1

Name _____

-ed words

Write each word three times.

bed

fed

led

red

wed

Ted

Phonics, KS1

Name _____   -ed words

Find the words on Silly Sea Serpent. Write them on the lines below.

1 _____   2 _____   3 _____

4 _____   5 _____   6 _____

41

Copyright © 1996 Brighter Vision Education Ltd   Phonics, KS1

Name _____   -ed words

Unscramble the words.

db e _____

dr e _____

ed w _____

de f _____

dl e _____

dT e _____

Now draw pictures of these words.

| fed | bed | red |

42

Name _____

—et words

Help Otto Octopus make words.

1 _____
2 _____
3 _____
4 _____
5 _____
6 _____

Hi kids!

n g s p w j et

Colour the rhyming fish.

set net get leg wet pet jet bed ten

Name _____

—et words

Write each word three times.

get

jet

net

pet

set

wet

Name _____

–et words

Find the words on Silly Sea Serpent. Write them on the lines below.

1 _____

2 _____

3 _____

4 _____

5 _____

6 _____

Start here

Name _____   —et words

Unscramble the words.

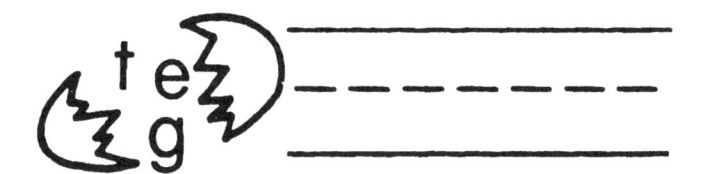

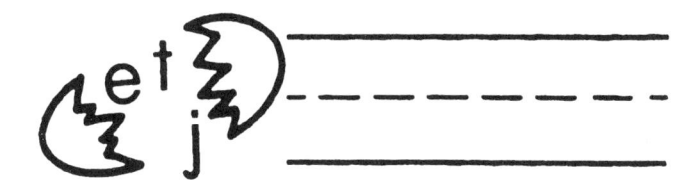

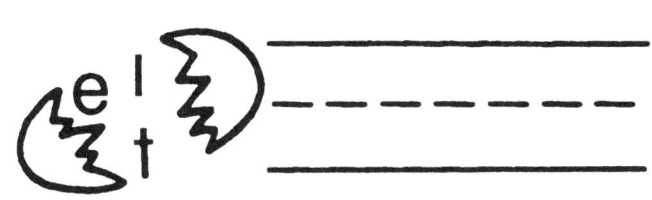

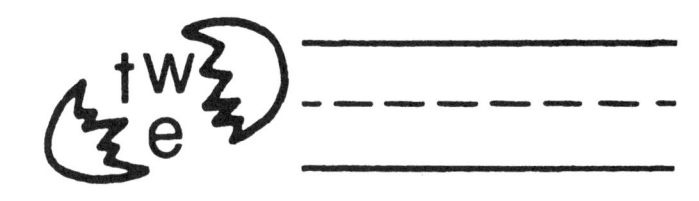

t e g _____

e t j _____

e l t _____

e p t _____

t w e _____

e s t _____

Now draw pictures of these words.

| jet | pet | wet |

46

Copyright © 1996 Brighter Vision Education Ltd   Phonics, KS1

Name _____ —it words

Help Otto Octopus make words.

1 _____ 2 _____ 3 _____

4 _____ 5 _____ 6 _____

"Hi kids!"

k b h p f s —it

Colour the rhyming fish.

kit hip pit pin fig hit sit bit fit

47

Copyright © 1996 Brighter Vision Education Ltd   Phonics, KS1

Name _____ —it words

Write each word three times.

tit

fit

hit

sit

kit

Name _____ — it words

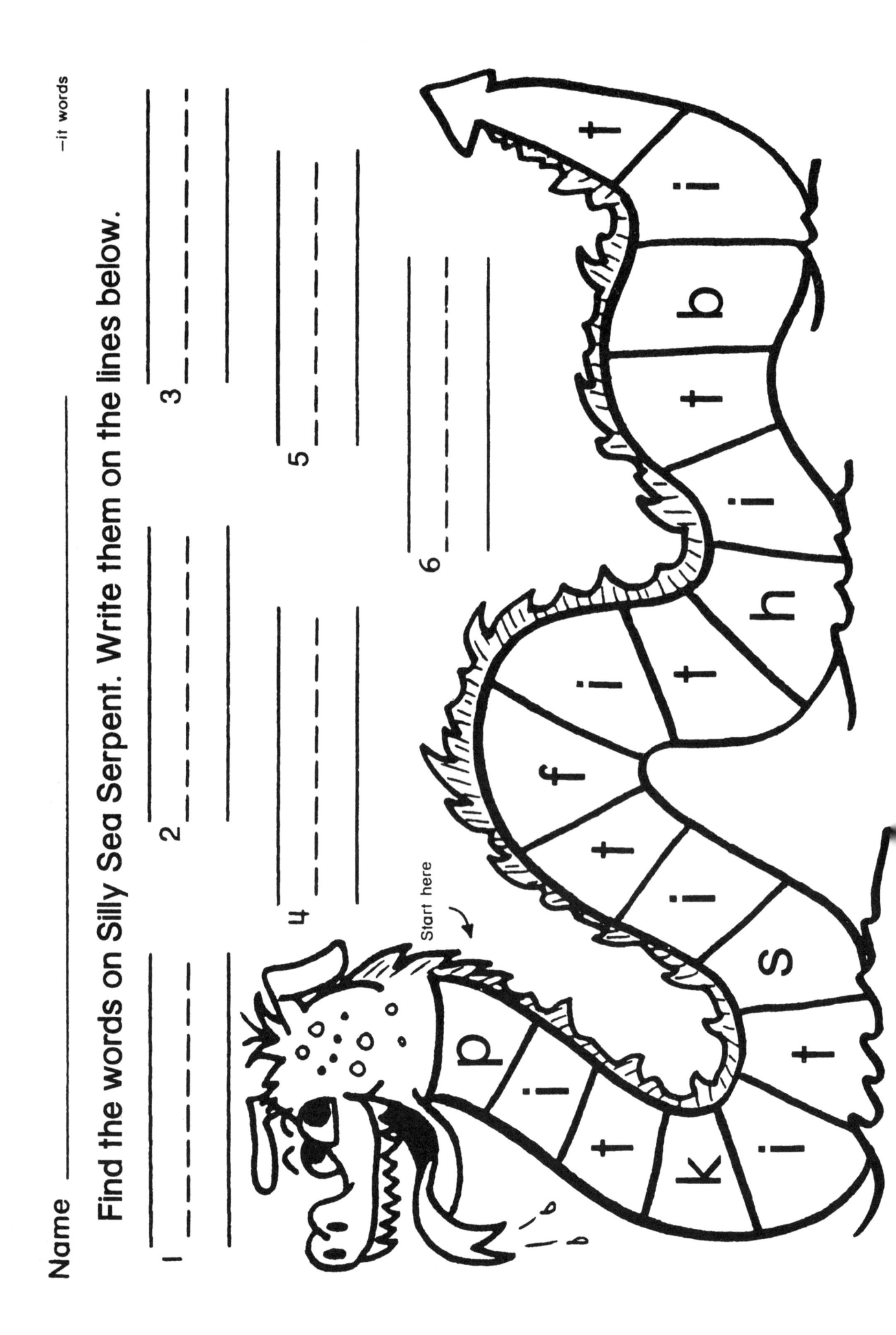

Find the words on Silly Sea Serpent. Write them on the lines below.

1. _____
2. _____
3. _____
4. _____
5. _____
6. _____

Name _____ —it words

Unscramble the words.

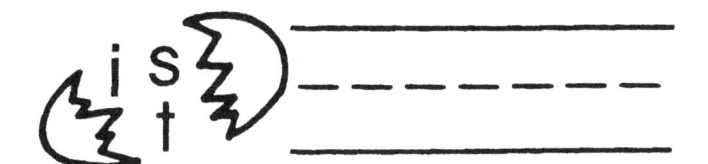

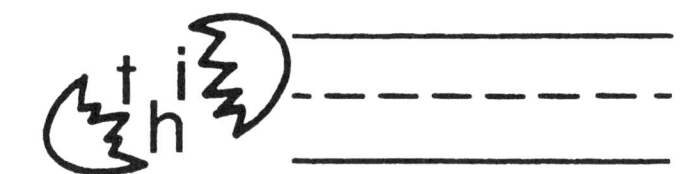

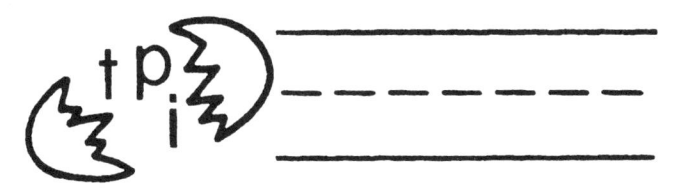

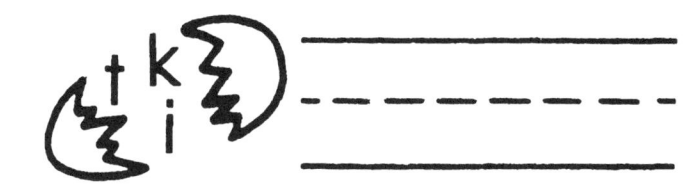

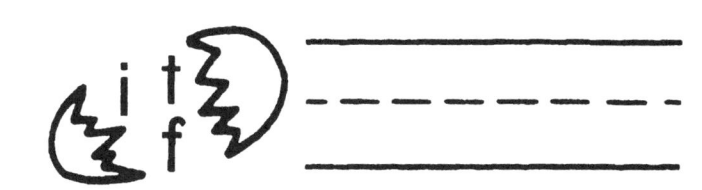

is t _____

t h i _____

t p i _____

i t b _____

t k i _____

i t f _____

Now draw pictures of these words.

| kit | pit | lit |

50

Name _____ —ig words

Help Otto Octopus make words.

Hi kids!

f
d
b
ig
p
w

1 _____
2 _____
3 _____
4 _____
5 _____

Colour the rhyming fish.

hid • fit • pin • pig • fig • dig • wig • big • tip

Copyright © 1996 Brighter Vision Education Ltd   Phonics, KS1

Name _____ —ig words

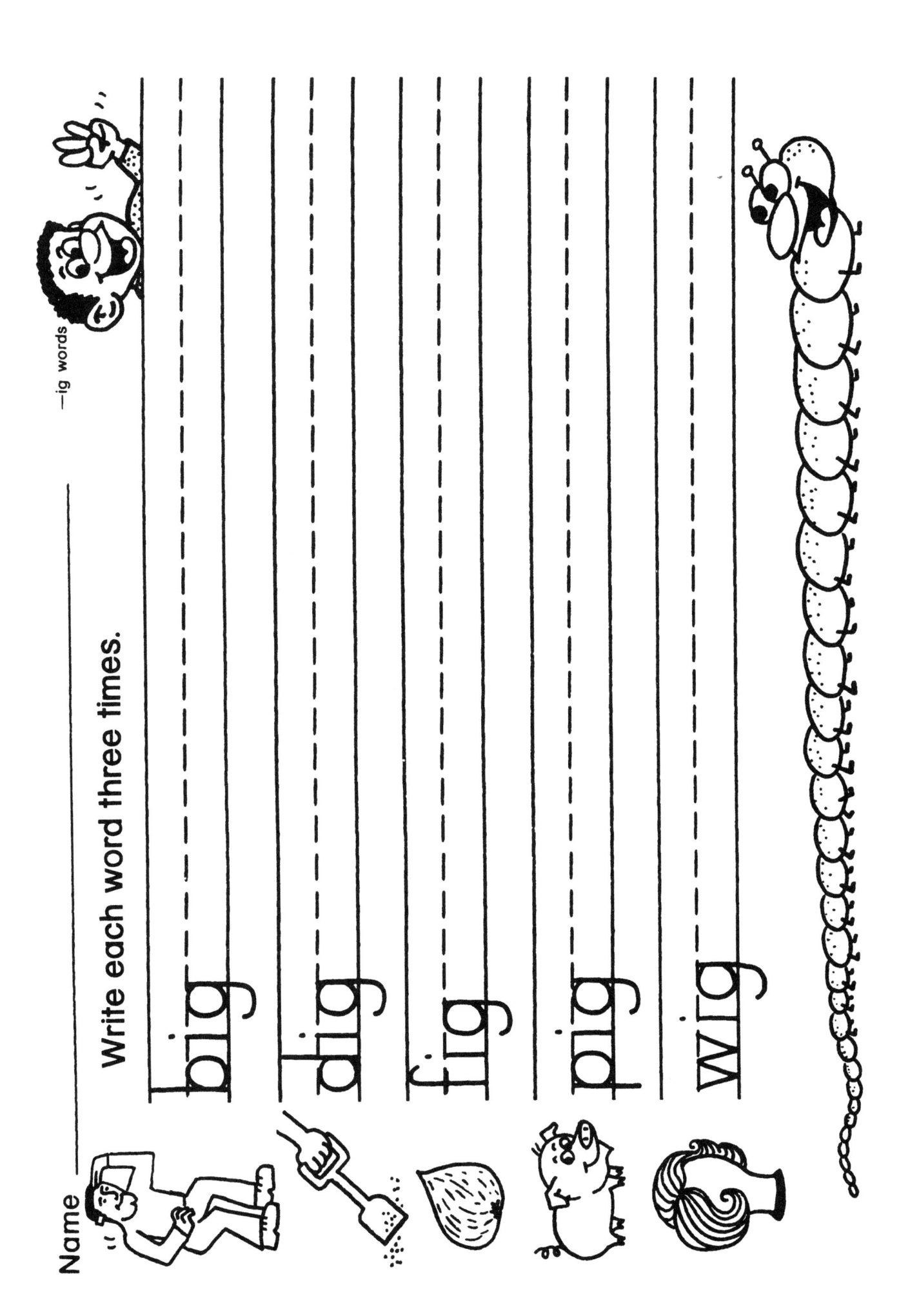

Write each word three times.

big _____ _____

dig _____ _____

fig _____ _____

pig _____ _____

wig _____ _____

Name _____ —ig words

Find the words on Silly Sea Serpent. Write them on the lines below.

1 _____
2 _____
3 _____
4 _____
5 _____

Start here

p i g
b i g
d i g
f i g
w i g

53

Copyright © 1996 Brighter Vision Education Ltd   Phonics, KS1

Name _____   —ig words

Unscramble the words.

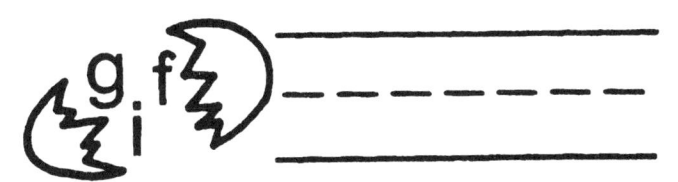

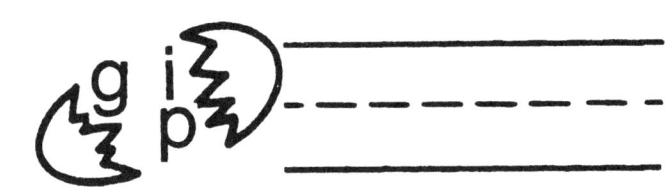

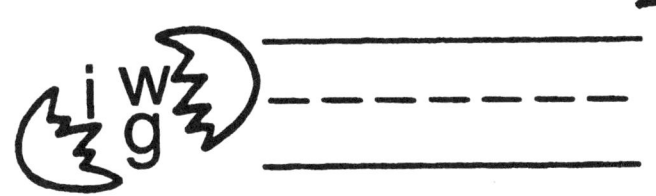

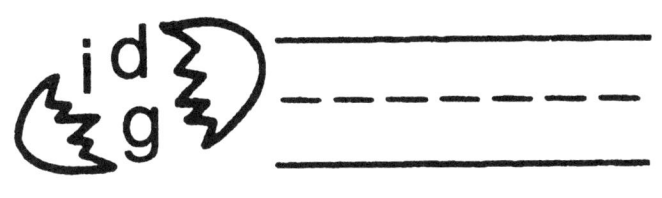

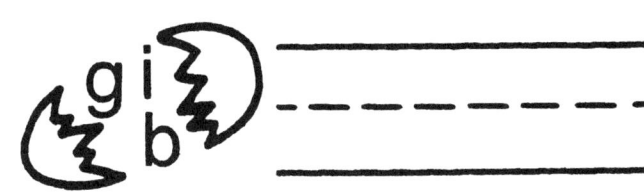

g i f _____

g i p _____

i w g _____

i d g _____

g i b _____

Now draw pictures of these words.

| pig | wig | fig |

Name _____ —ip words

Help Otto Octopus make words.

1 _____ 2 _____
3 _____ 4 _____
5 _____ 6 _____

Hi kids!

Colour the rhyming fish.

55

Copyright © 1996 Brighter Vision Education Ltd   Phonics, KS1

Name _____ —ip words

Write each word three times.

dip

hip

lip

rip

sip

tip

Copyright © 1996 Brighter Vision Education Ltd   Phonics, KS1

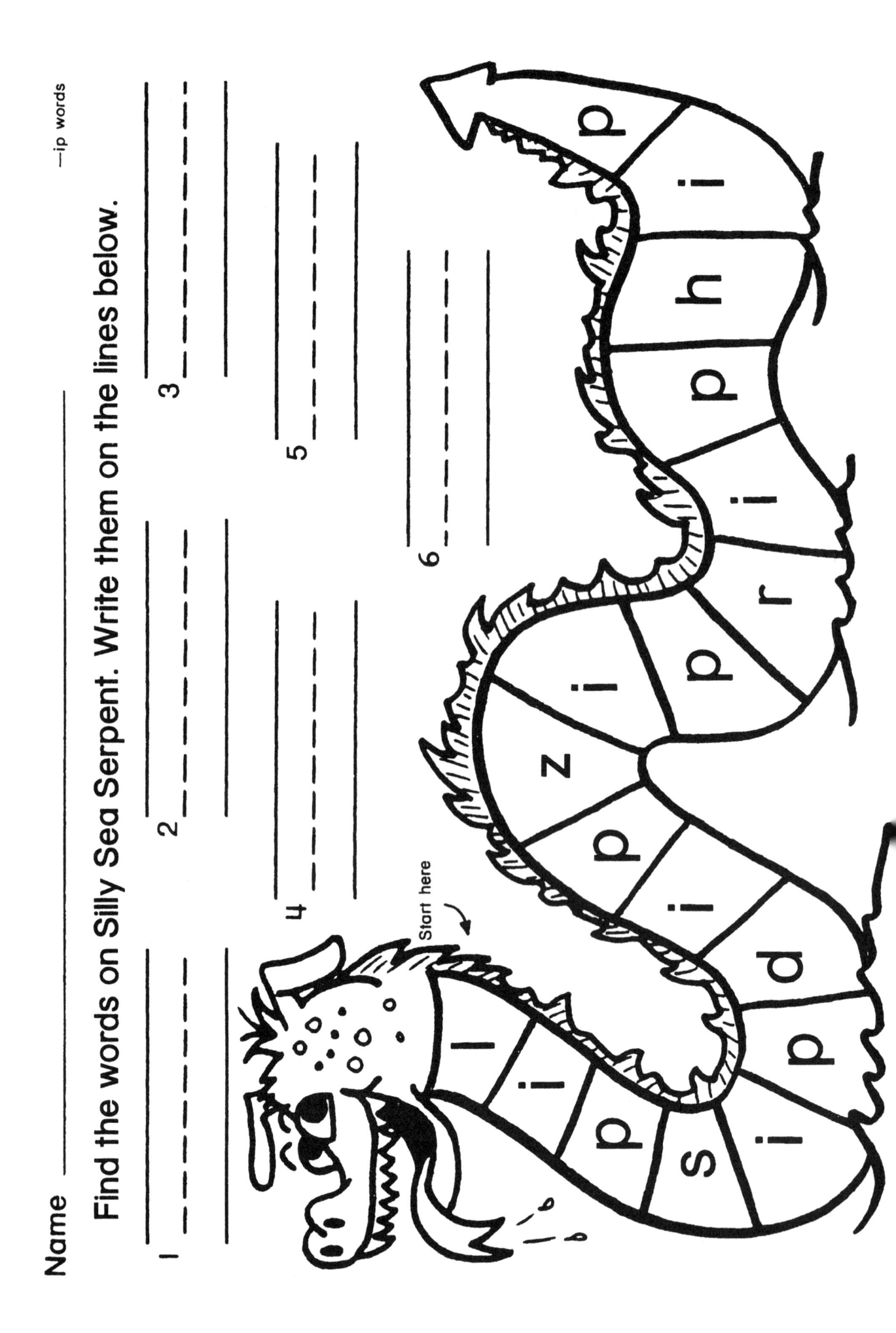

Name _____ —ip words

Find the words on Silly Sea Serpent. Write them on the lines below.

1 _____

2 _____

3 _____

4 _____

5 _____

6 _____

Name _____   —ip words

Unscramble the words.

p h i — _____

p i r — _____

i s p — _____

p i d — _____

i l p — _____

i p z — _____

Now draw pictures of these words.

| lip | rip | hip |

58

Name _____

—og words

Help Otto Octopus make words.

1 __ __ __
2 __ __ __
3 __ __ __
4 __ __ __
5 __ __ __

Hi kids!

og

d f h j l

Colour the rhyming fish.

fog job log dog mop pod hog jog not

Name _____ —og words

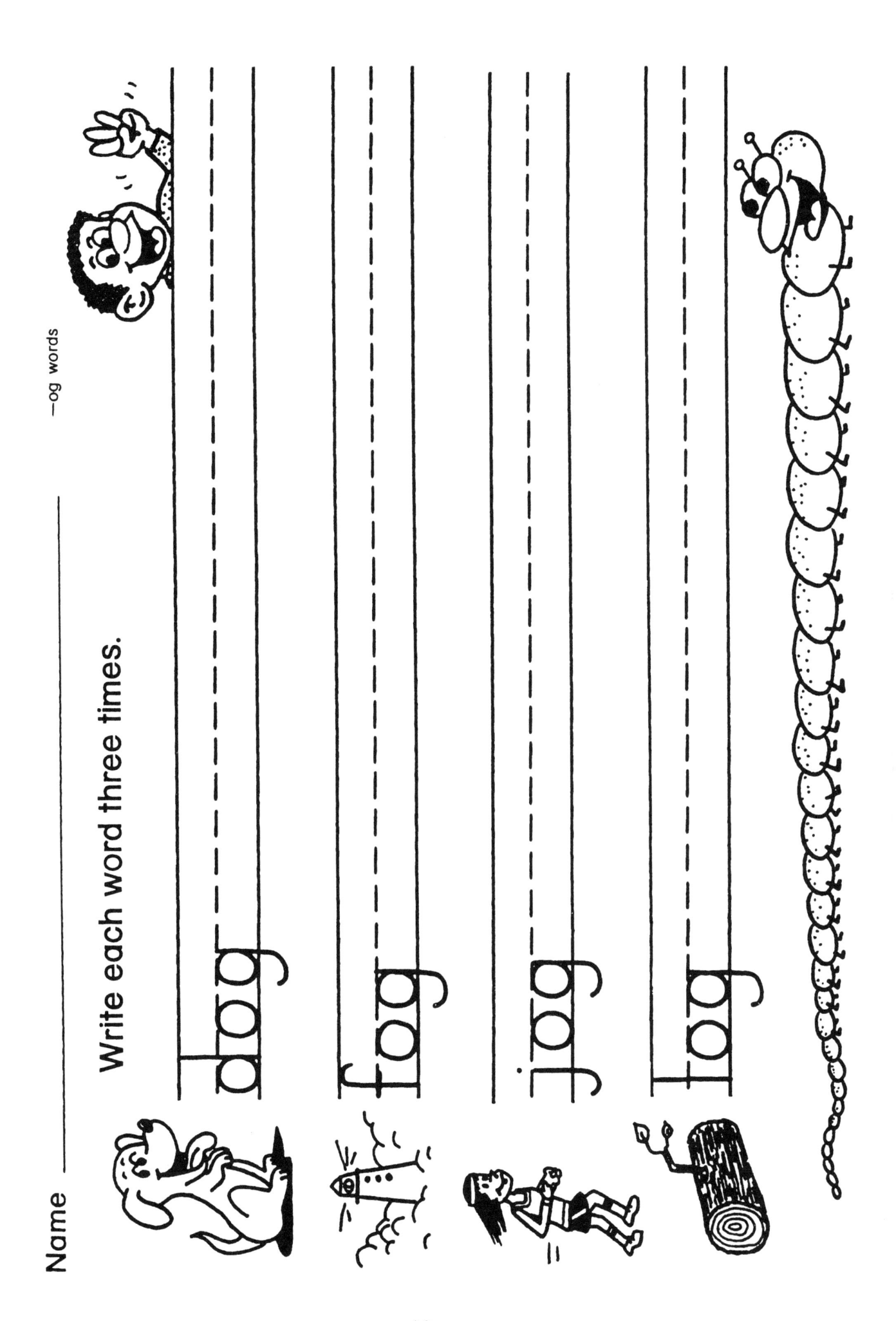

Write each word three times.

dog

fog

jog

log

Name _____ —og words

Find the words on Silly Sea Serpent. Write them on the lines below.

1 _____

2 _____

3 _____

4 _____

5 _____

Name _____   —og words

Unscramble the words.

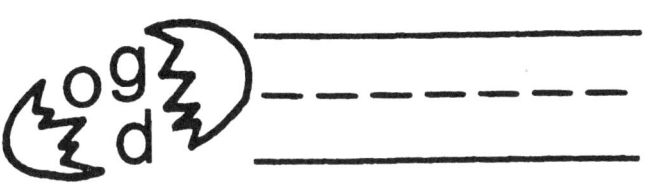

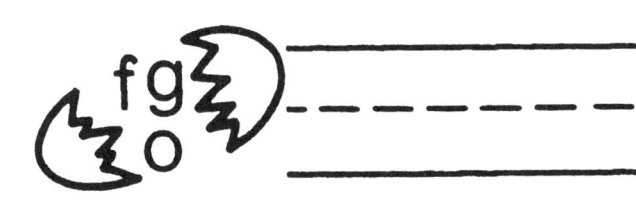

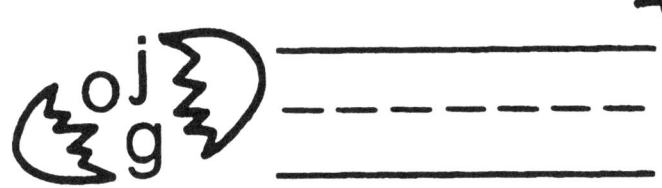

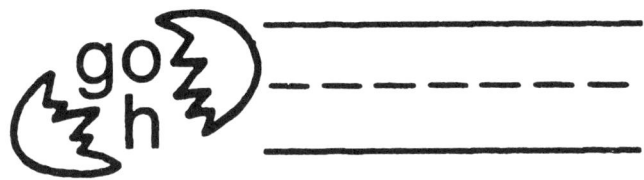

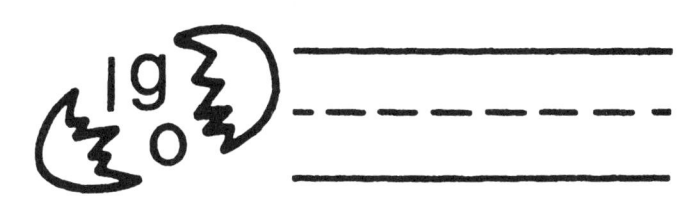

og
d   _ _ _ _ _ _

fg
o   _ _ _ _ _ _

oj
g   _ _ _ _ _ _

go
h   _ _ _ _ _ _

lg
o   _ _ _ _ _ _

Now draw pictures of these words.

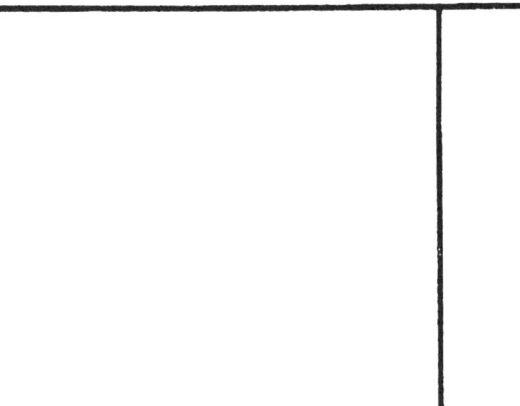

dog	jog	log

62

Name _____

—op words

Help Otto Octopus make words.

1 _____

2 _____

3 _____

4 _____

Hi kids!

op
t p m h

Colour the rhyming fish.

sob   dot   jog   top   mop   pop   nod   hop

63

Copyright © 1996 Brighter Vision Education Ltd

Phonics, KS1

Name _____   —op words

Write each word three times.

hop ---------- ----------

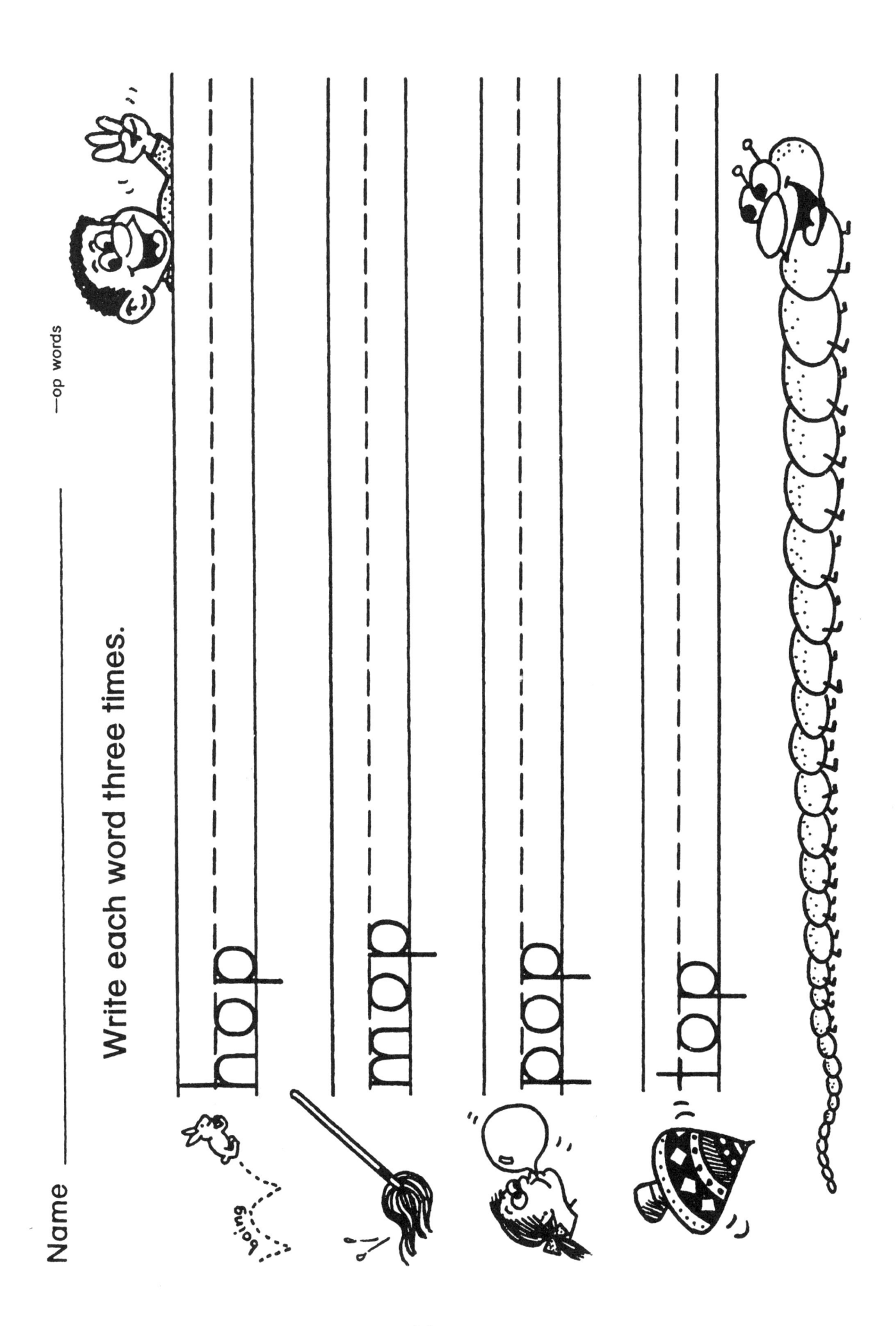

mop ---------- ----------

pop ---------- ----------

top ---------- ----------

Name _____ —op words

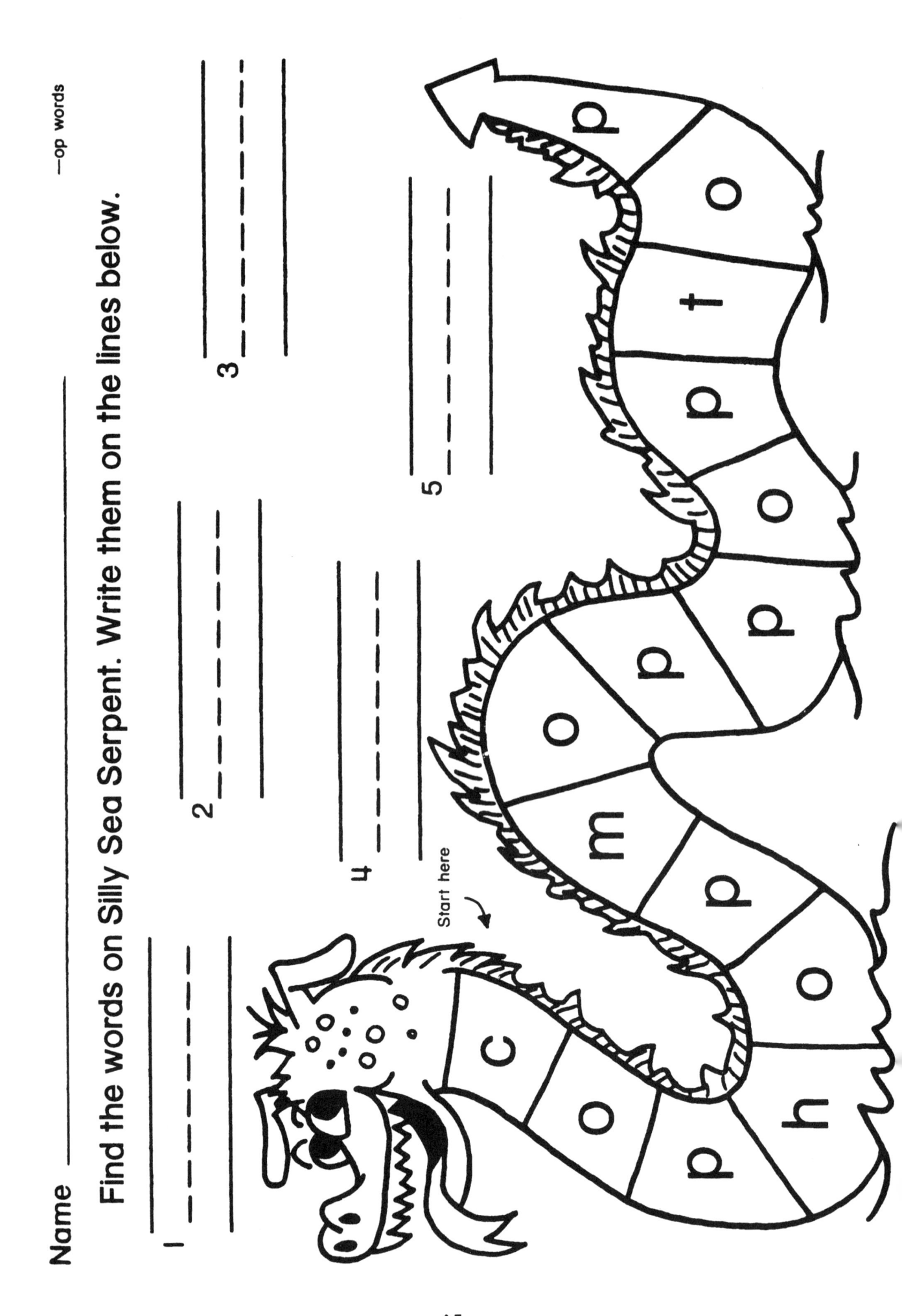

Find the words on Silly Sea Serpent. Write them on the lines below.

1 _____

2 _____

3 _____

4 _____

5 _____

Name _____   —op words

Unscramble the words.

o p h _ _ _ _ _ _ _

p o m _ _ _ _ _ _ _

p p o _ _ _ _ _ _ _

o p t _ _ _ _ _ _ _

Now draw pictures of these words.

top	mop	hop

Name _____

—ot words

Help Otto Octopus make words.

1 _____ 2 _____

3 _____ 4 _____

5 _____ 6 _____

Hi kids!

c d g h n p ot

Colour the rhyming fish.

hot pop got dot rod not pot fog cot

67

Copyright © 1996 Brighter Vision Education Ltd

Phonics, KS1

Name _____ —ot words

Write each word three times.

cot

got

dot

hot

not

pot

Name _____ —ot words

Find the words on Silly Sea Serpent. Write them on the lines below.

1 _____ 2 _____ 3 _____

4 _____ 5 _____ 6 _____

Name _____   —ot words

Unscramble the words.

c o t _____

t d o _____

o g t _____

h t o _____

o t n _____

t o l _____

Now draw pictures of these words.

| dot | cot | hot |

70

Copyright © 1996 Brighter Vision Education Ltd   Phonics, KS1

Name _____

—ub words

Help Otto Octopus make words.

1 ___
2 ___
3 ___
4 ___
5 ___

"Hi kids!"

c r s t h ub

Colour the rhyming fish.

cub   fun   tub   cup   sub   hub   cut   bug   rub

71

Copyright © 1996 Brighter Vision Education Ltd

Phonics, KS1

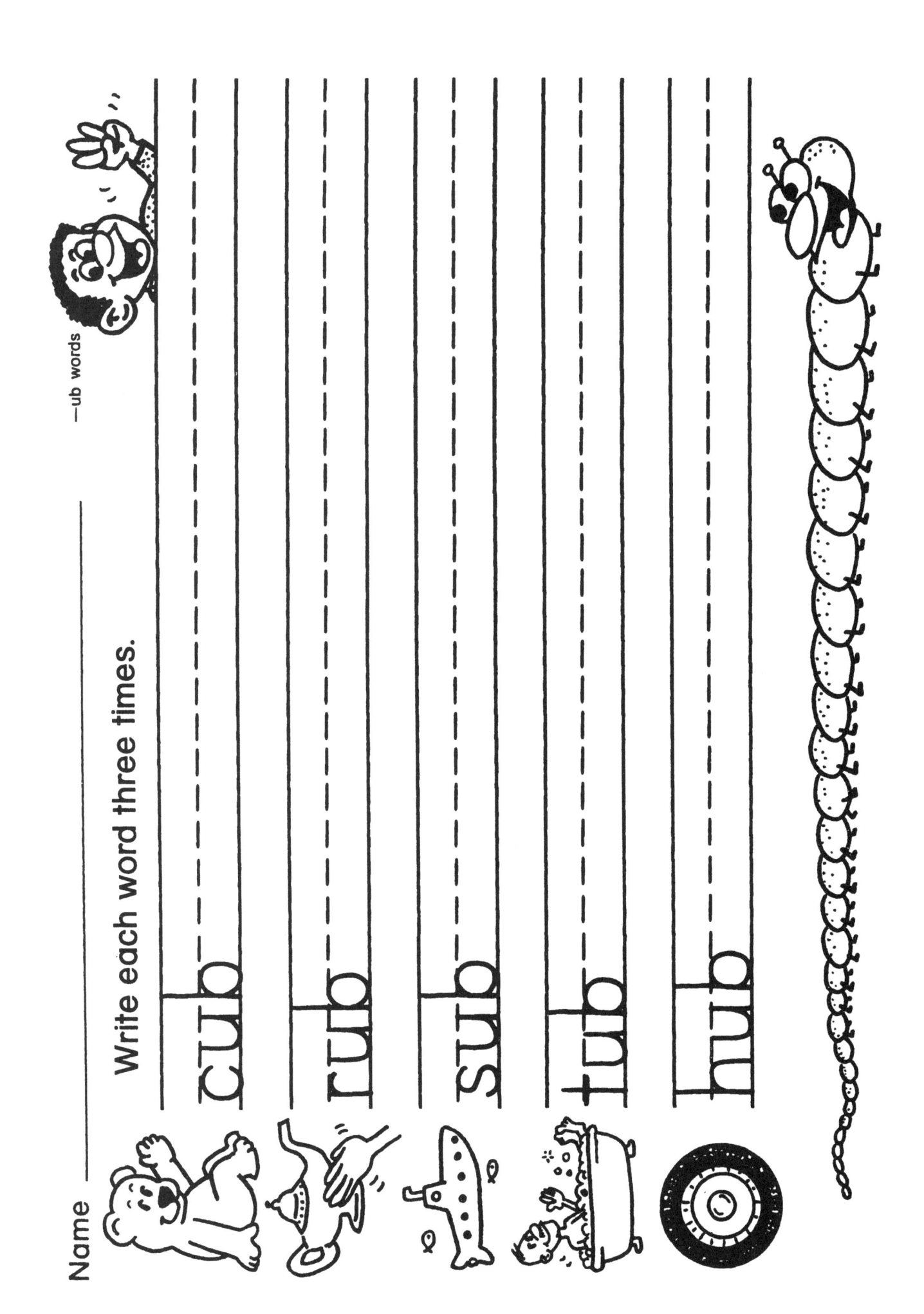

Name _____

—ub words

Write each word three times.

cub

rub

sub

tub

hub

Name _____ —ub words

Find the words on Silly Sea Serpent. Write them on the lines below.

1 _____

2 _____

3 _____

4 _____

5 _____

Name _____ —ub words

Unscramble the words.

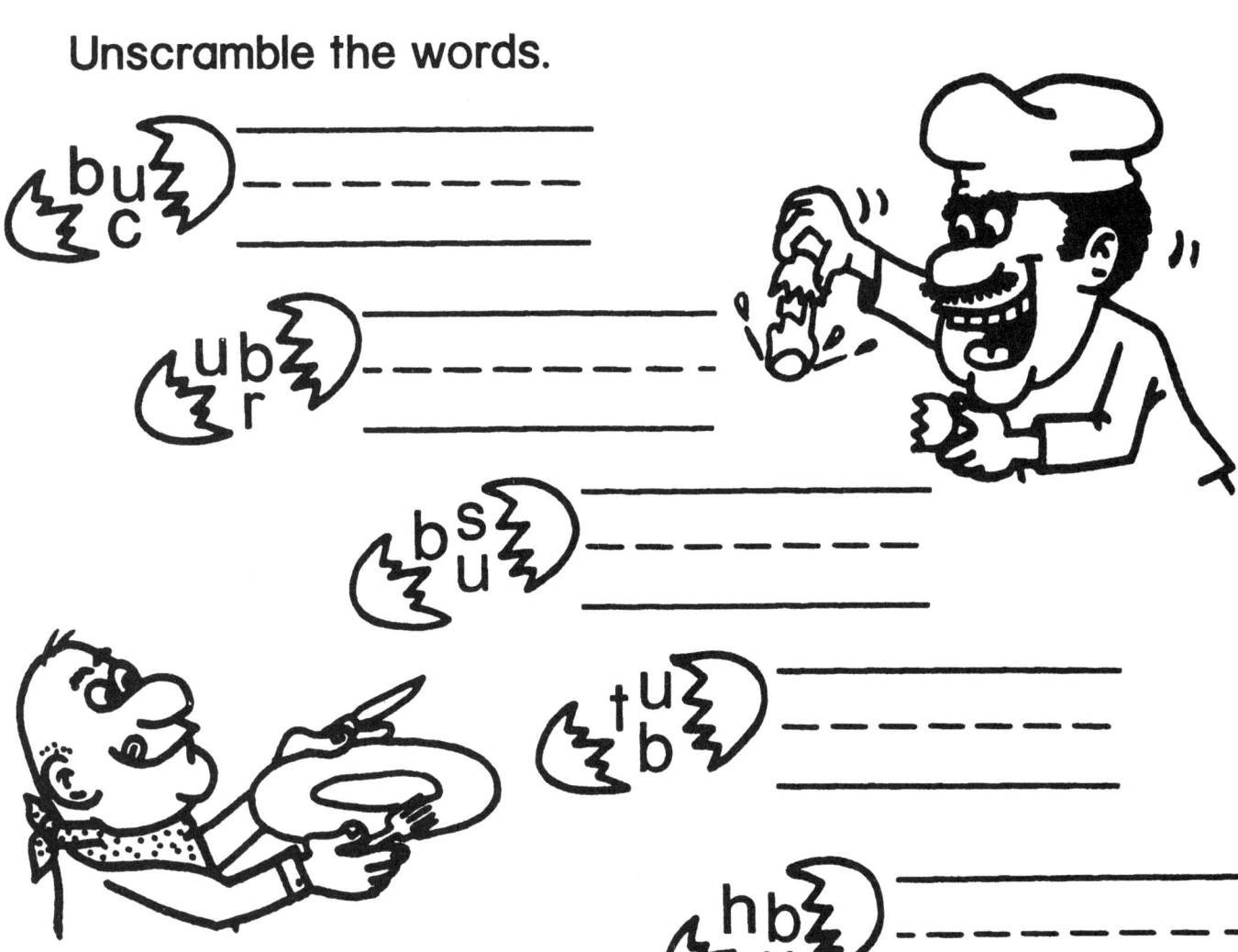

bu c _____

ub r _____

b s u _____

t u b _____

h b u _____

Now draw pictures of these words.

| cub | sub | tub |

74

Copyright © 1996 Brighter Vision Education Ltd Phonics, KS1

Name _____ —un words

Help Otto Octopus make words.

1. _____
2. _____
3. _____
4. _____
5. _____

Hi kids!

b un s r n f

Colour the rhyming fish.

tub   nun   bun   fun   rug   sun   hut   run

75

Copyright © 1996 Brighter Vision Education Ltd   Phonics, KS1

Name ———————

—un words

Write each word three times.

bun

fun

run

sun

nun

76

Copyright © 1996 Brighter Vision Education Ltd

Phonics, KS1

Name _____

—un words

Find the words on Silly Sea Serpent. Write them on the lines below.

1 _____ 2 _____ 3 _____

4 _____ 5 _____

77

Copyright © 1996 Brighter Vision Education Ltd

Phonics, KS1

Name _____ —un words

Unscramble the words.

n u b _____

f n u _____

r n u _____

u s n _____

n n u _____

Now draw pictures of these words.

| nun | sun | bun |

Name _____ —ug words

Help Otto Octopus make words.

1. _____ 2. _____
3. _____ 4. _____
5. _____ 6. _____

"Hi kids!"

b t r m h d ug

Colour the rhyming fish.

rug, cut, mug, sub, bug, hug, tug, dug, sun

Name _____ —ug words

Write each word three times.

dug

hug

mug

rug

tug

Name _____   –ug words

Find the words on Silly Sea Serpent. Write them on the lines below.

1 _____   2 _____   3 _____

4 _____   5 _____   6 _____

Start here

b-u-g   p-u-g   h-u-g   j-u-g   r-u-g   t-u-g

81

Copyright © 1996 Brighter Vision Education Ltd   Phonics, KS1

Name _____ —ug words

Unscramble the words.

ub g _____

gu d _____

hg u _____

u J g _____

ur g _____

gu t _____

Now draw pictures of these words.

| bug | jug | tug |

Name _____   Review of short vowels
                                       a, i

Print the missing vowel.

m__n	p__n	s__x
c__n	w__g	b__t
c__p	f__n	k__ng
l__d	h__nd	h__ll

83

Copyright © 1996 Brighter Vision Education Ltd   Phonics, KS1

Name _____   Review of short vowels
                                         a, i

Print the vowel you hear in each picture.

Name _____   Review of short vowels
a, i

pin	fat	tip
pan	lip	tap
fit	lap	

Fill in the blanks with words.

1	These don't _____ .
2	I sat on a _____ !
3	I am so _____ .
4	I have a new _____ .
5	Spot is in my _____ .

Name _____ Review of short vowels
a, i

Print the correct word on each apple.

1. I see a _____ .
   bat, bit

2. That van is _____ .
   bag, big

3. Kim is _____ .
   sack, sick

4. Sam filled the _____ .
   pan, pin

5. The girl ate some _____ .
   ham, him

6. Pat has a blue _____ .
   rang, ring

Colour the apples that have short **a** words red.

Colour the apples that have short **i** words green.

Name _____   Review of short vowels
i, o

hot	dig	pop
hit	jog	pig
dog	big	

Fill in the blanks with words.

1 	You look _____ .
2 	I _____ every day.
3 	Pinky is my pet _____ .
4 	Tiny is my pet _____ .
5 	It might _____ .

87

Copyright © 1996 Brighter Vision Education Ltd   Phonics, KS1

Review of short vowels
a, u

Name _____

cat	but	hat
cut	fan	hut
bat	fun	

Fill in the blanks with words.

1	I want to, _____ I can't.
2	I have a pet _____ .
3	That is a _____ .
4	Ow! I have a _____ .
5	Turn on the _____ .

Name _____

Review of short vowels
o, u

not	sun	run
hug	dot	hop
top	bug	

Fill in the blanks with words.

1		I _____ fast!
2		I am _____ a boy.
3		I love the _____ .
4		Mum gave me a _____ .
5		See my new _____ !

89

Copyright © 1996 Brighter Vision Education Ltd

Phonics, KS1

Name _____ Review of short vowels
a, i, o

Print the missing vowel.

 p__n	 d__g	 h__t
 p__t	 r__ng	 m__p
 m__t	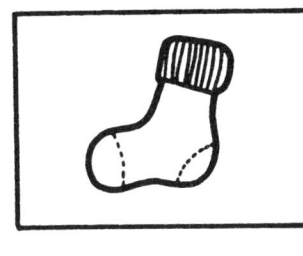 s__ck	 c__n
 f__sh	 t__ck	 l__g

90

Copyright © 1996 Brighter Vision Education Ltd Phonics, KS1

Name _____   Short vowels **e, o, u**

Fill in the blanks with **e**, **o**, or **u**.

1. A rabbit can h___p.

2. A h___n sat on some eggs.

3. A d___ck was in the water.

4. An insect has six l___gs.

5. A p___p likes to play.

6. A f___x can run fast.

7. A fish was in the n___t.

8. A cat sat on a b___x.

9. A pig was in the m___d.

10. A rat was on my d___sk.

Circle the sentence that is about the picture above. In the box, draw another picture of one of the other sentences.

Name _____   Review of short vowels
a, i, o, u

Print the missing vowel.

 b__x	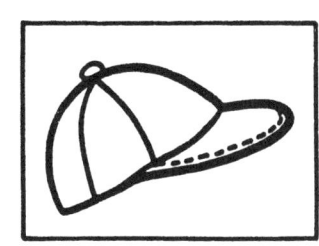 c__p	 s__n
 r__ng	 d__ll	 f__n
 t__p	 l__g	 s__x
 b__t	 p__n	 c__p

92

Copyright © 1996 Brighter Vision Education Ltd   Phonics, KS1

Name _____ Review of short vowels
a, i, o, u

Print the vowel you hear in each picture.

Name _____

Review of short vowels
a, e, i, o, u

Circle the vowel sound you hear in each word.

 6 — a e i	 cap — e i a	 
 net — a e i	 sun — e u o	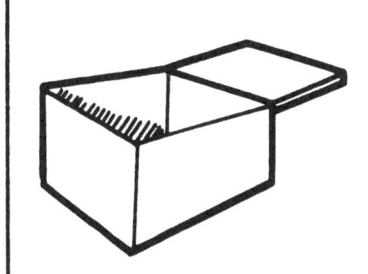 box — o e a
 fan — a e i	 web — i a e	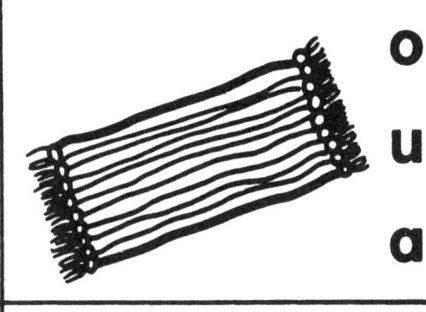 mat — o u a
 hat — a e i	 tent — a i e	 fish — e i a
 nuts — u o i	 mop — u o e	 can — e a u

94

Copyright © 1996 Brighter Vision Education Ltd

Phonics, KS1

Name _____ Review of short vowels
a, e, i, o, u

Print the missing vowel.

 j_t	 s_n	 m_p
 p_n	 t_p	 t_ck
 l_g	 n_t	 p_g
 d_ll	 b_t	 t_n

95

Copyright © 1996 Brighter Vision Education Ltd Phonics, KS1

Name _____   Review of short vowels
a, e, i, o, u

Print the vowel you hear in each picture.

Name _____

Review of short vowels
a, e, i, o, u

Circle the word for each picture.

	 pan pen pin		 fan fin fun		 lag log lug
	 net not nut		 hat hit hut		 pat pet pot
	 sack sick sock		 tan ten tin		 lick lock luck
	 rang ring rung		 lamp limp lump		 ball bell bill

97

Copyright © 1996 Brighter Vision Education Ltd

Phonics, KS1

Name _____

Short vowels
a, e, i, o, u

Circle the word for each picture.

hat / hit / hut	cat / cot / cut	hat / hot / hut
deck / dock / duck	pan / pen / pin	dig / dog / dug
rang / ring / rung	bat / bet / but	lick / lock / luck
sack / sick / sock	lamp / limp / lump	ball / bell / bill

98

Copyright © 1996 Brighter Vision Education Ltd

Phonics, KS1

Answer Key

Page 1

Page 2

Page 3

Page 4

99

Copyright © 1996 Brighter Vision Education Ltd

Phonics, KS1

Answer Key

Name _____ Initial consonant **g**

Say the name of each picture. Write the beginning letter.

g g **g** g g g

Colour the pictures that begin with **g**.

Brainwork! Draw six pictures that begin with **g**.

Page 5

Name _____ Initial consonant **h**

Say the name of each picture. Write the beginning letter.

h h **h** h h h

Colour the pictures that begin with **h**.

Brainwork! Draw six pictures that begin with **h**.

Page 6

Name _____ Initial consonant **j**

Say the name of each picture. Write the beginning letter.

j j **j** j j j

Colour the pictures that begin with **j**.

Brainwork! Draw six pictures that begin with **j**.

Page 7

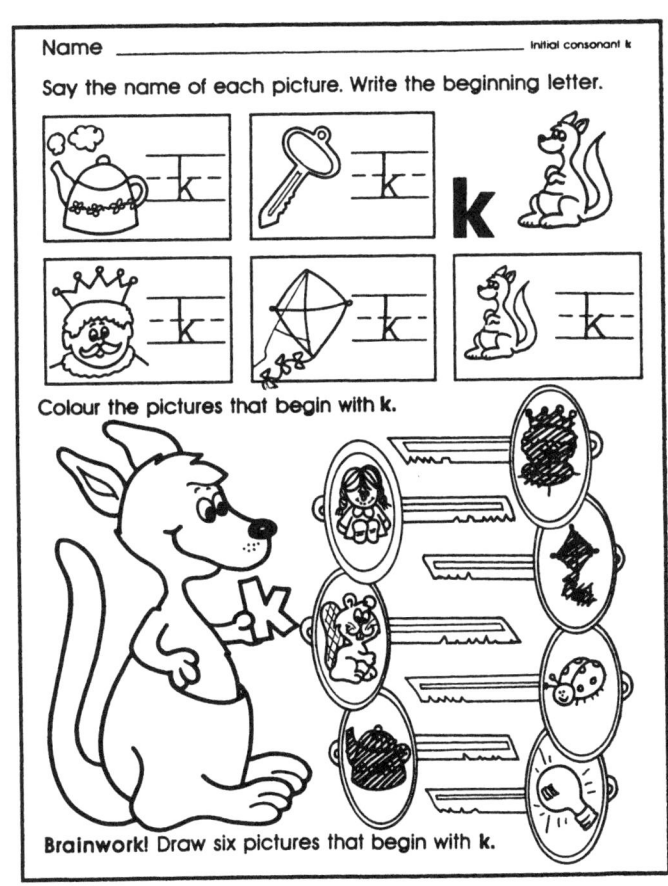

Name _____ Initial consonant **k**

Say the name of each picture. Write the beginning letter.

k k **k** k k k

Colour the pictures that begin with **k**.

Brainwork! Draw six pictures that begin with **k**.

Page 8

100

Copyright © 1996 Brighter Vision Education Ltd

Phonics, KS1

Answer Key

Page 9

Page 10

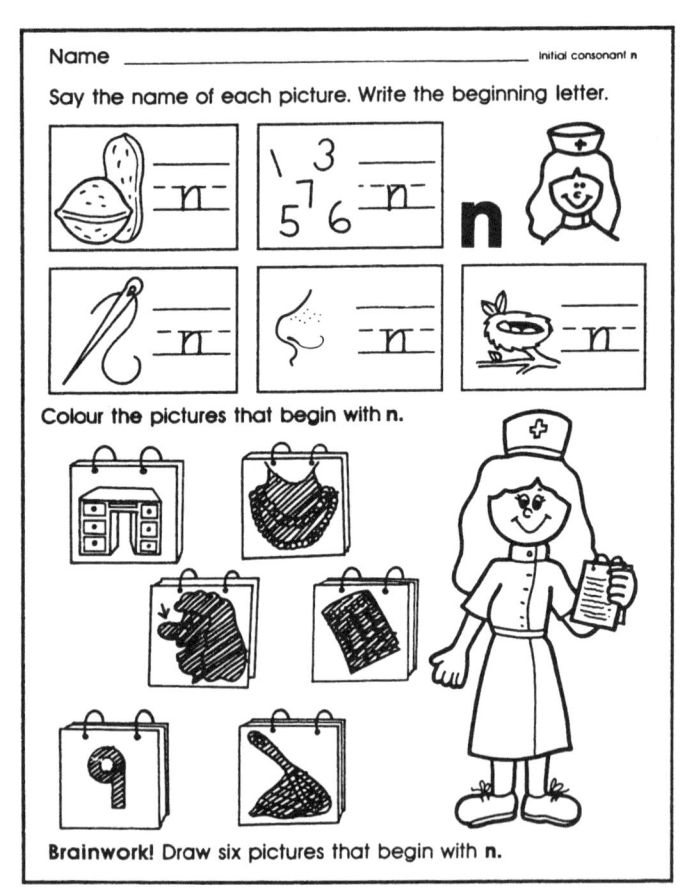

Page 11

Page 12

101

Answer Key

Page 13

Page 14

Page 15

Page 16

102

Copyright © 1996 Brighter Vision Education Ltd

Phonics, KS1

Answer Key

Page 17

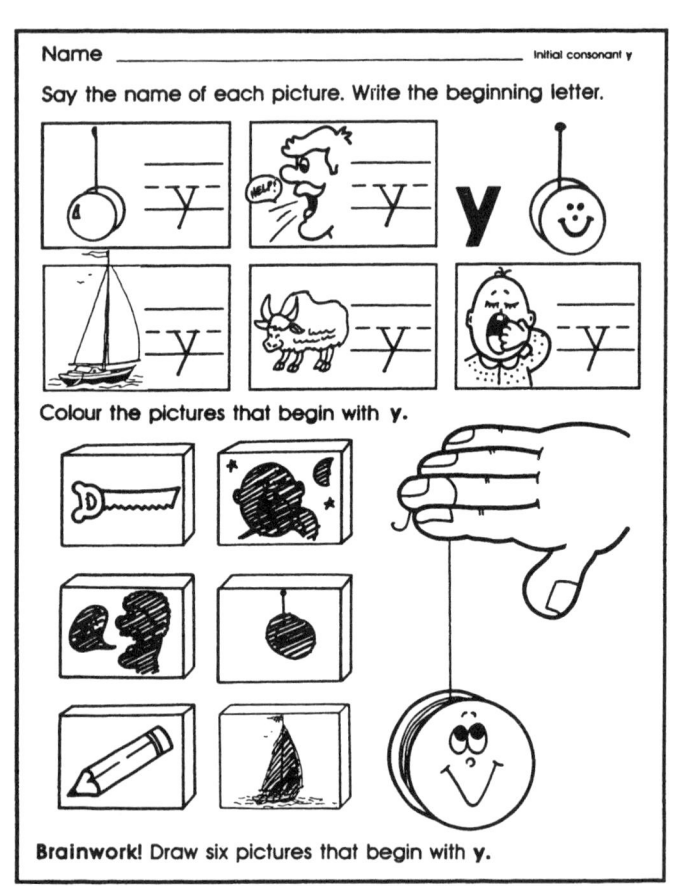

Page 18

Page 19

Page 20

103

Copyright © 1996 Brighter Vision Education Ltd

Phonics, KS1

Answer Key

Page 21

Print the beginning and ending letters.

bat	web	sun
six	box	hat
pot	fan	ten
hut	lid	top

Page 22

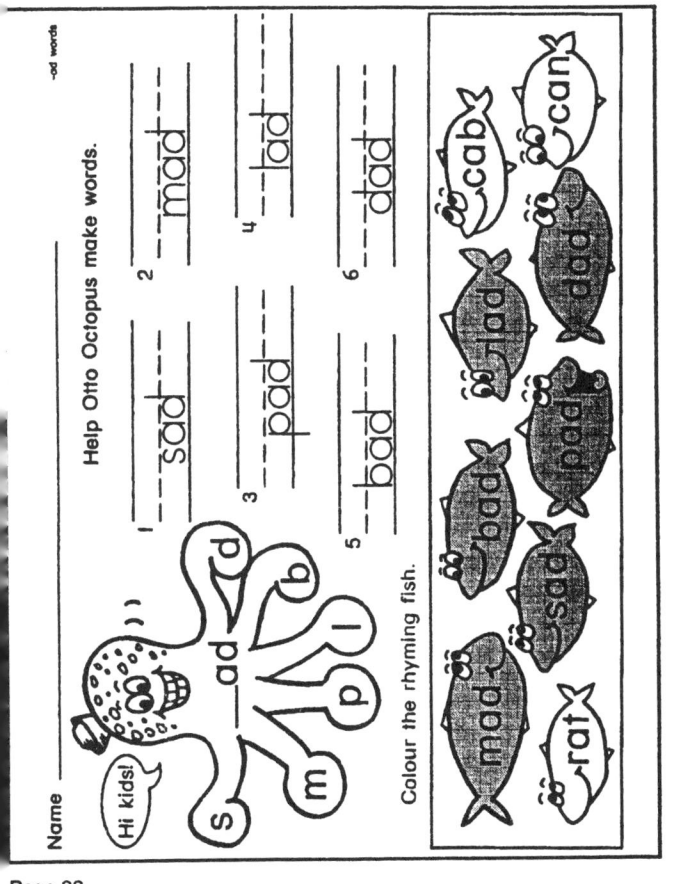

Use the pictures to finish the puzzle. The words go ↓ then →.

Across/Down: cat, top, pig, gum, open, web, bib, bag, gum, nut

Page 23

Help Otto Octopus make words.
1. sad
2. mad
3. bad
4. tad
5. bad
6. dad

Colour the rhyming fish: cab, can, mad, dad, pad, bad, sad (rat not coloured)

Page 24

Words are written as directed.
bad, dad, tad, sad

Answer Key

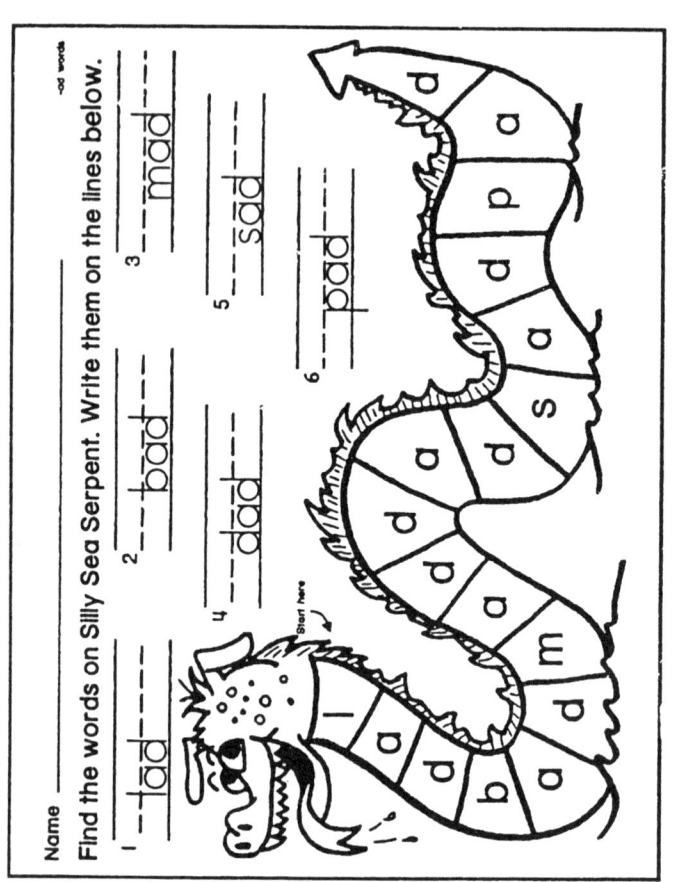

Page 25

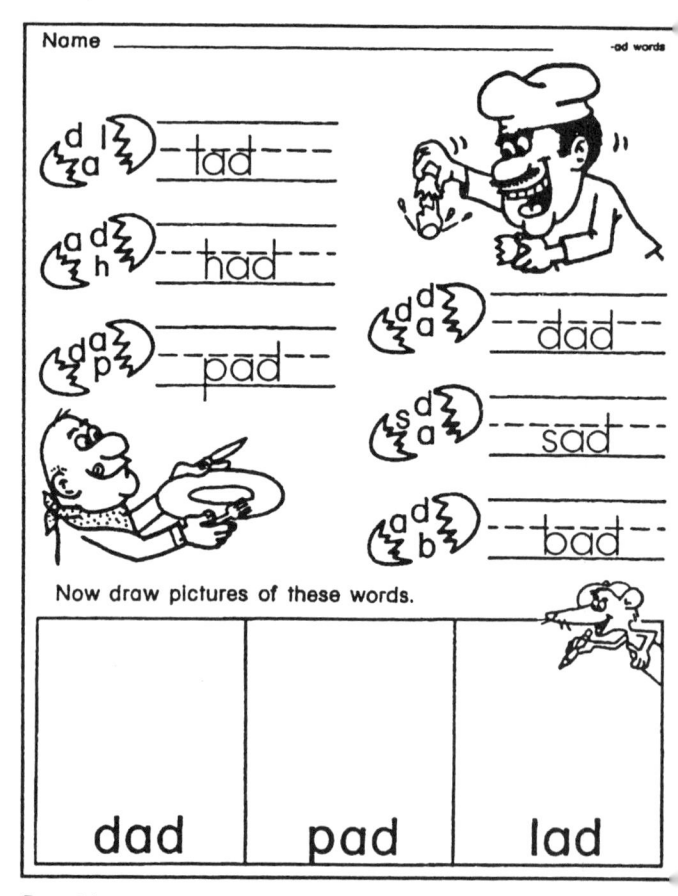

Page 26

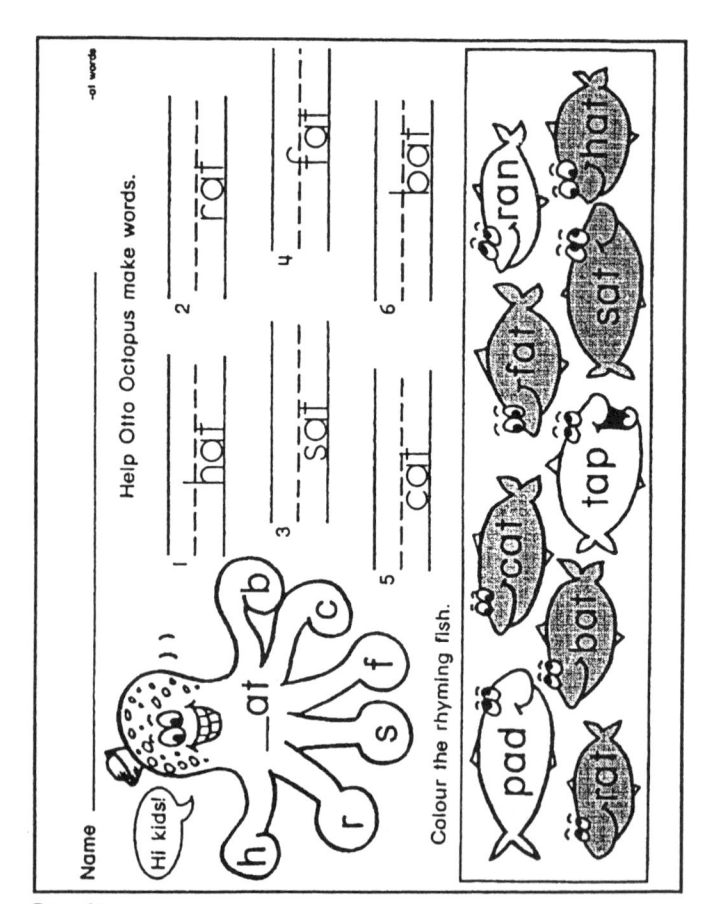

Page 27

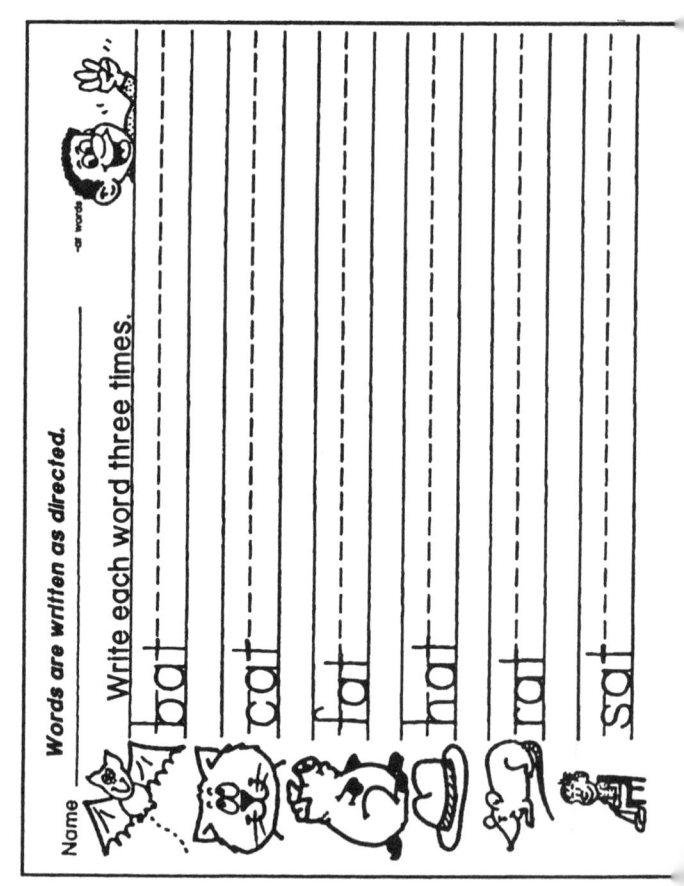

Page 28

105

Answer Key

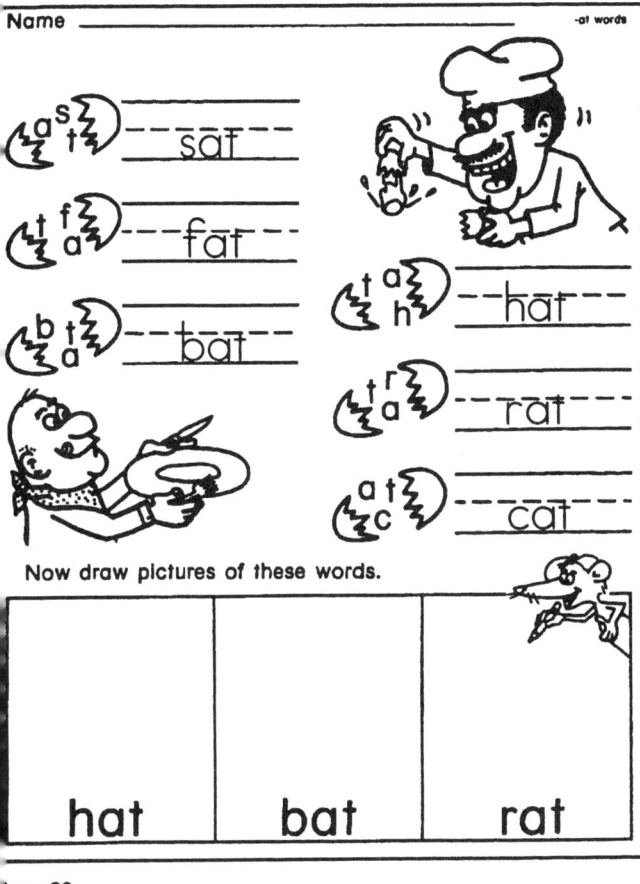

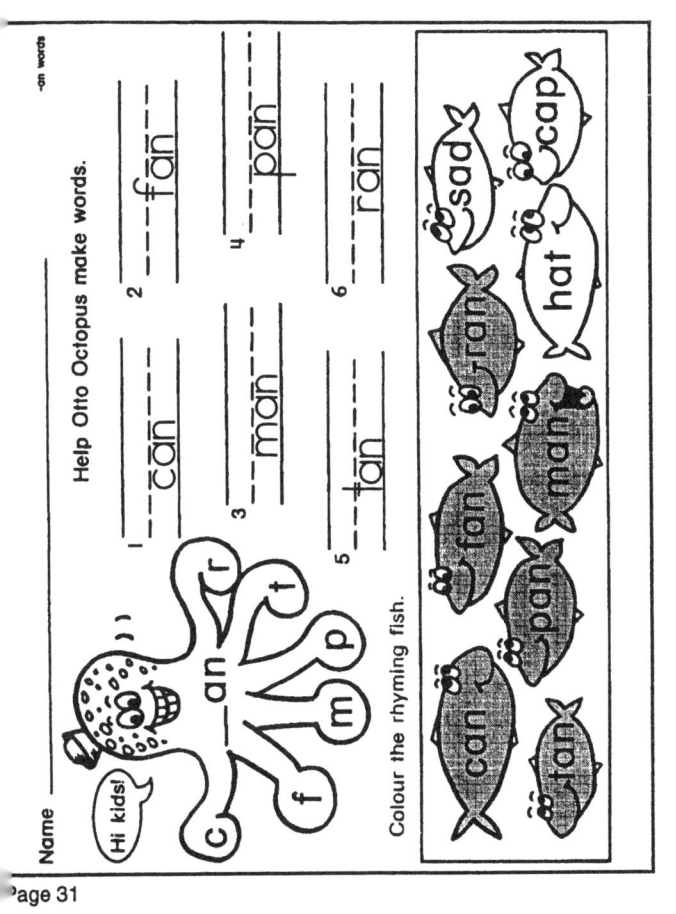

Page 29

Page 30

Page 31

Page 32

106

Answer Key

Page 33

Page 34

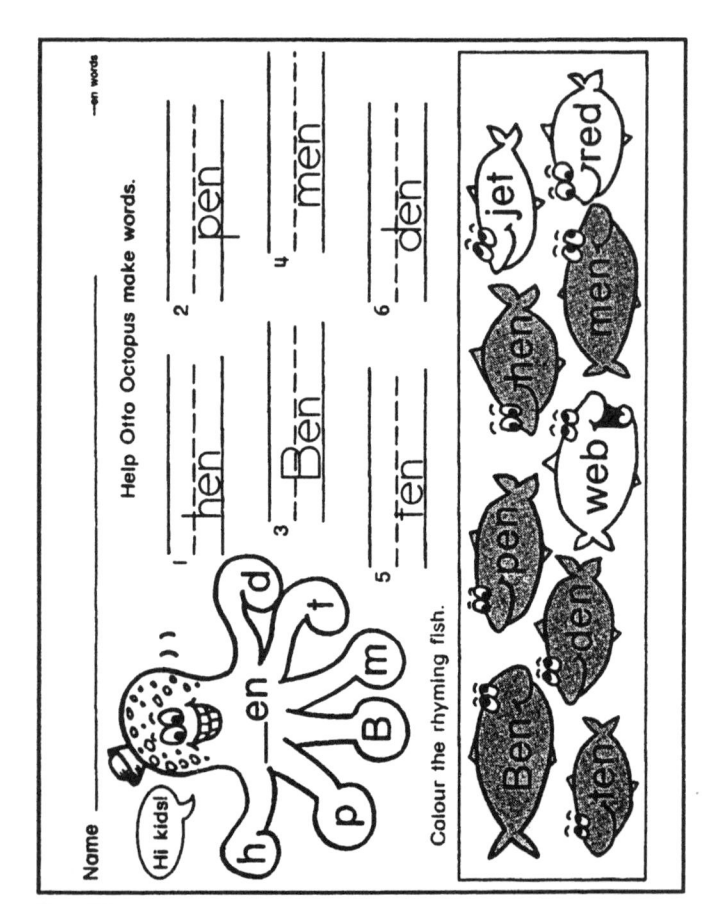

Page 35

Page 36

107

Answer Key

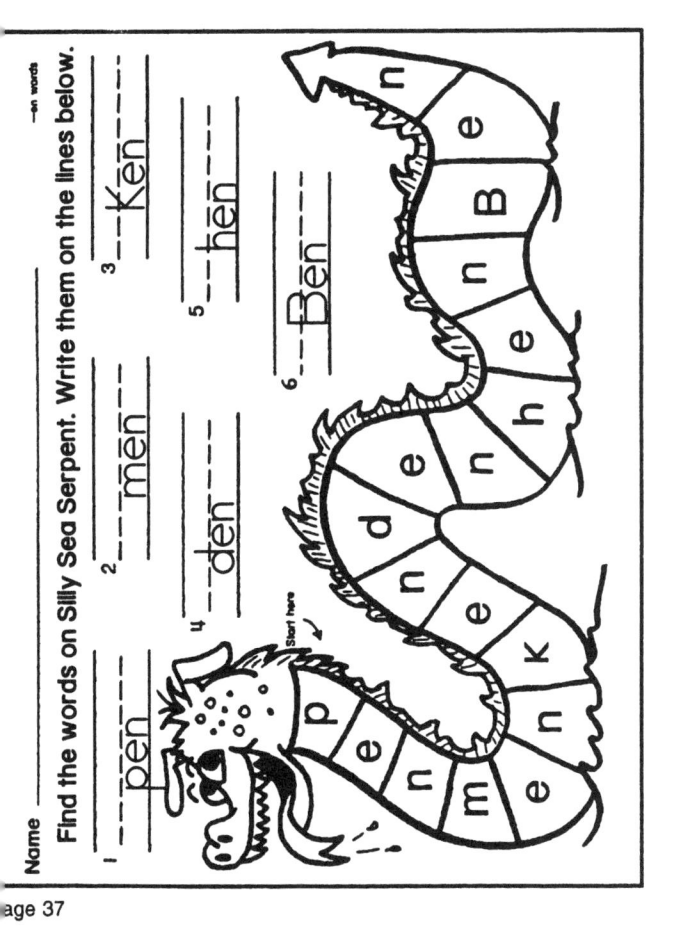

Page 37

Page 38

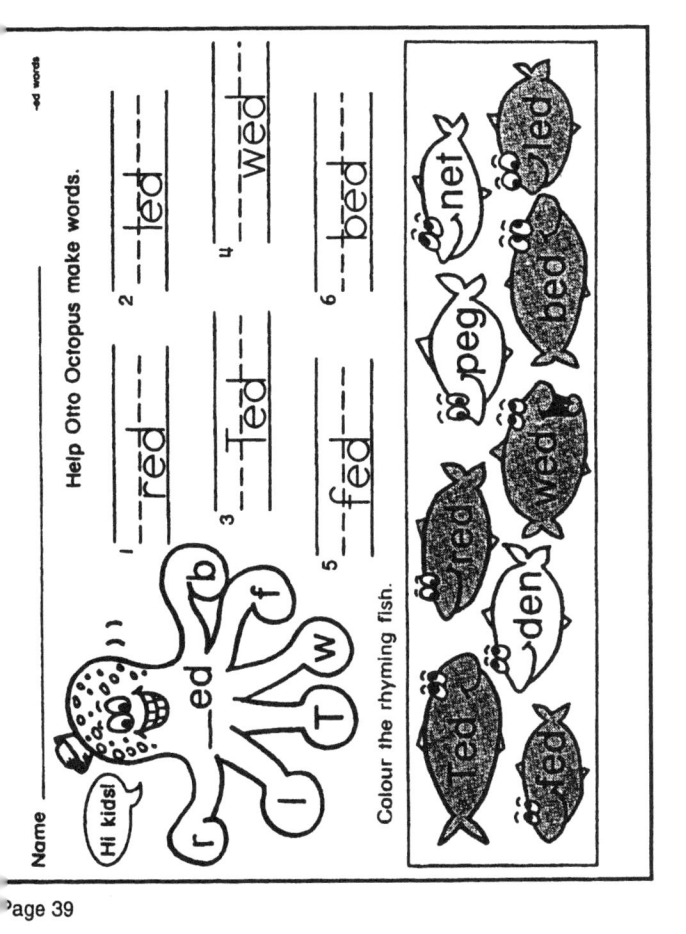

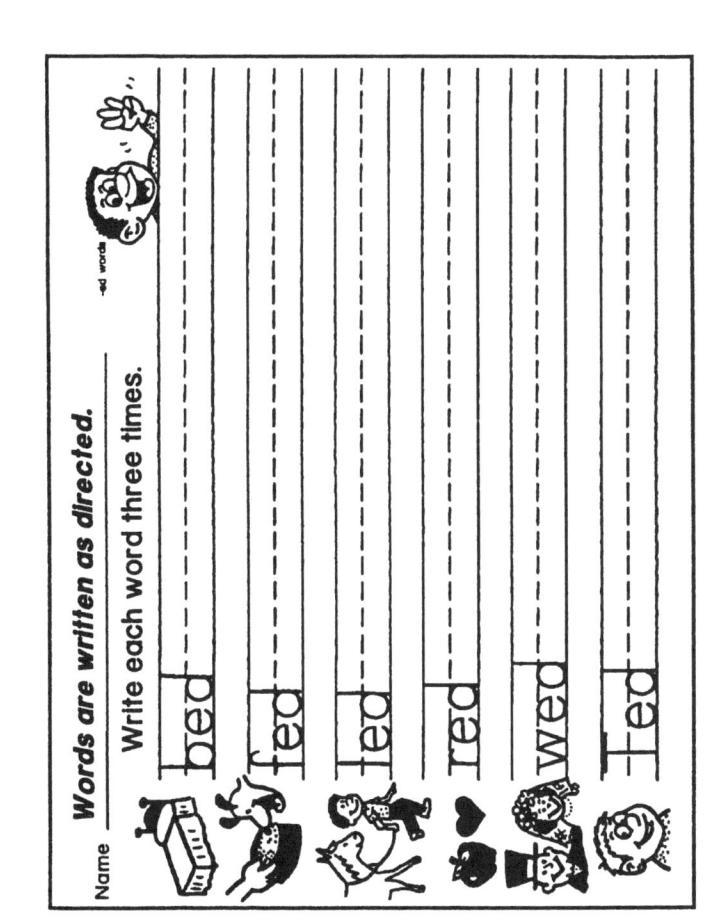

Page 39

Page 40

108

Answer Key

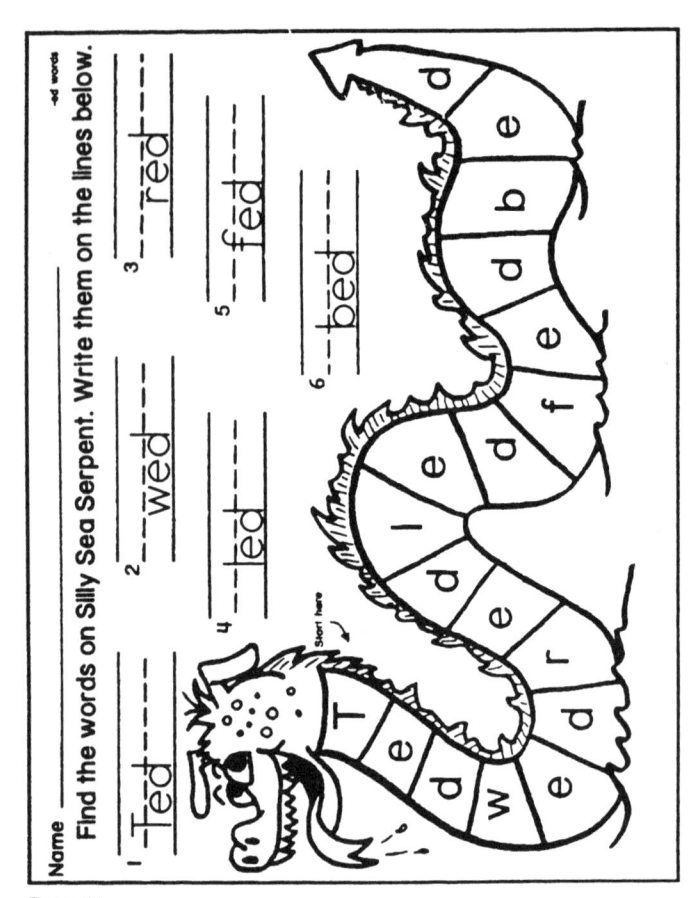

Page 41

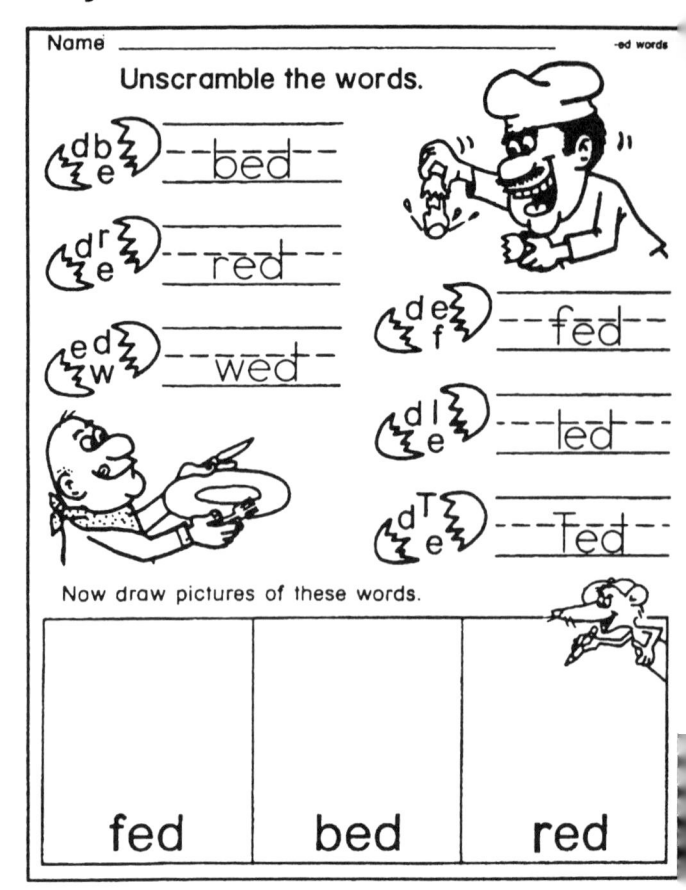

Page 42

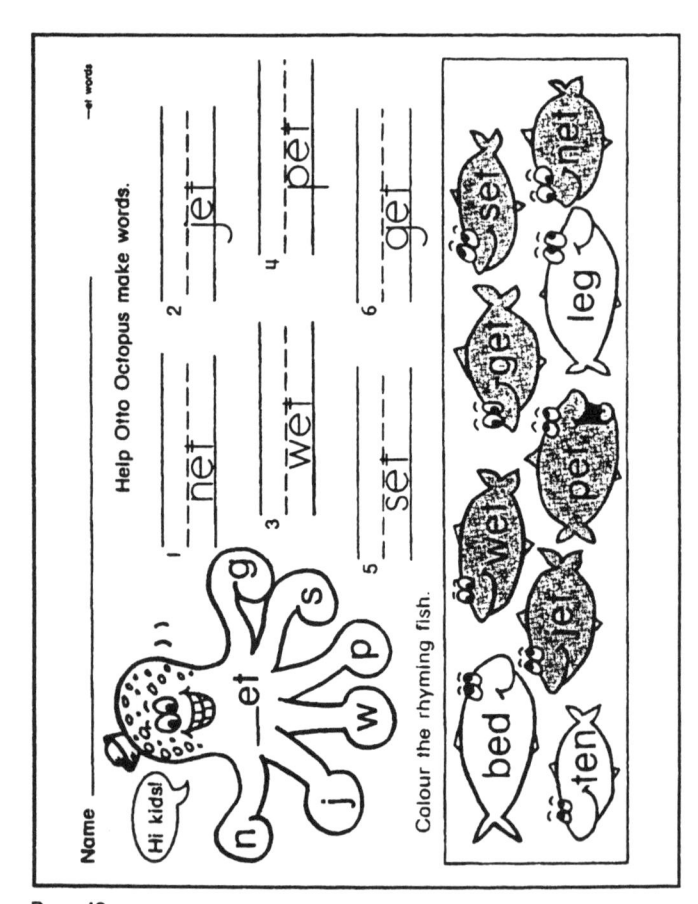

Page 43

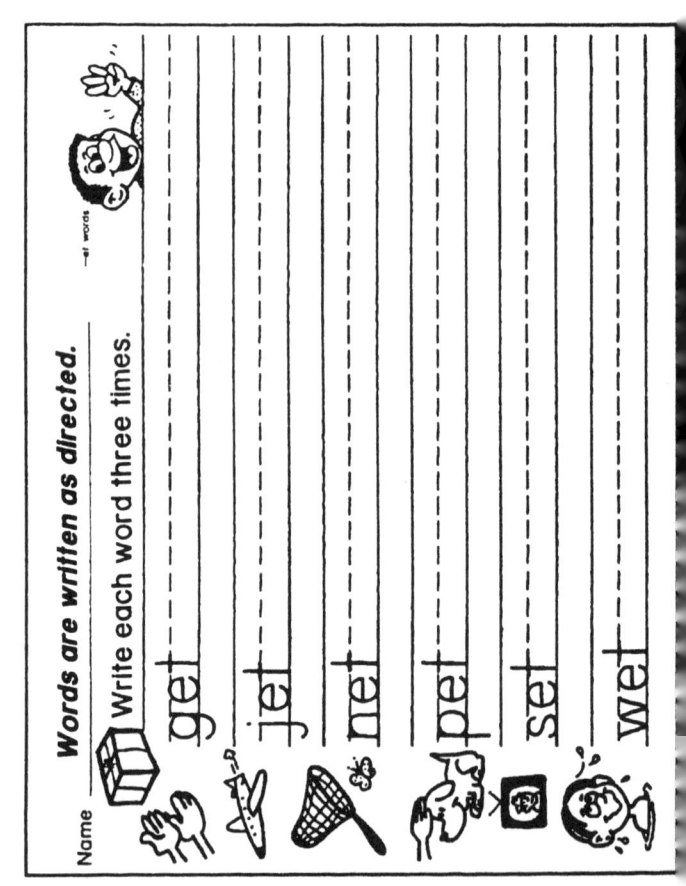

Page 44

109

Answer Key

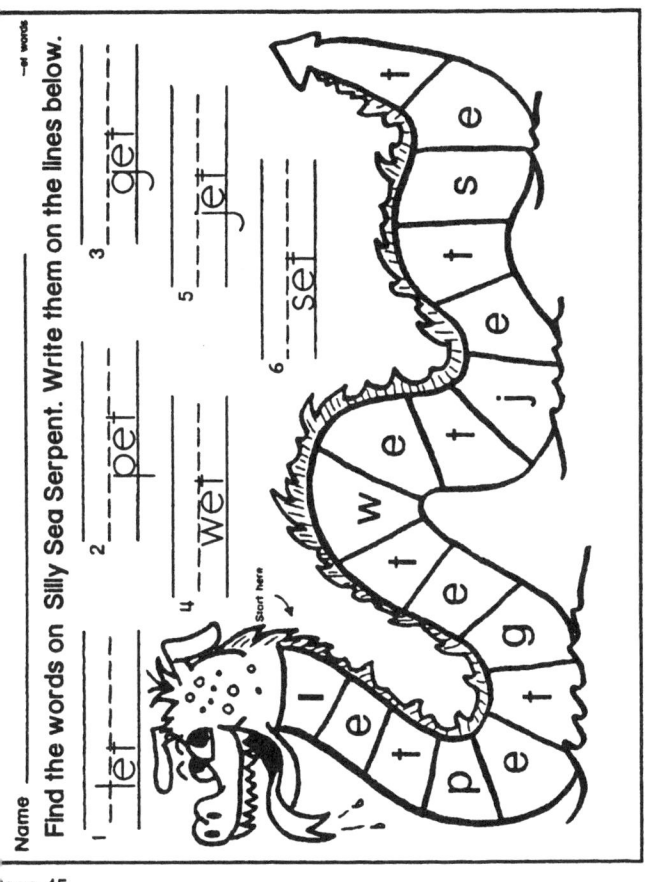

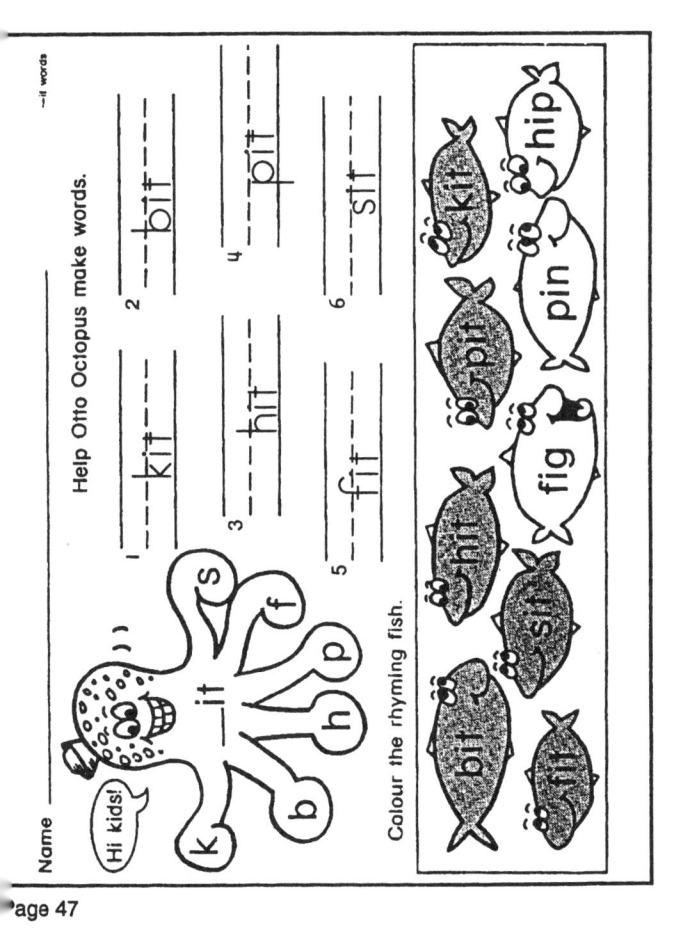

Page 45

Find the words on Silly Sea Serpent. Write them on the lines below.

1. let
2. pet
3. get
4. wet
5. jet
6. set

Page 46

Unscramble the words.

- get
- jet
- let
- pet
- wet
- set

Now draw pictures of these words.

| jet | pet | wet |

Page 47

Help Otto Octopus make words.

1. kit
2. bit
3. hit
4. pit
5. fit
6. sit

Colour the rhyming fish.

Page 48

Words are written as directed. Write each word three times.

- lit
- fit
- hit
- sit
- kit

Answer Key

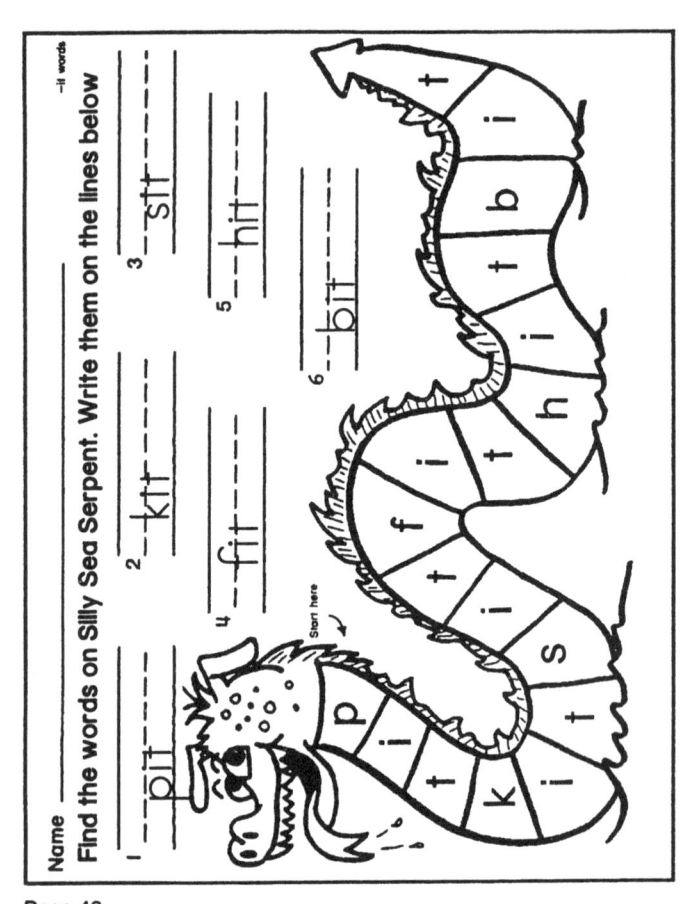

Page 49

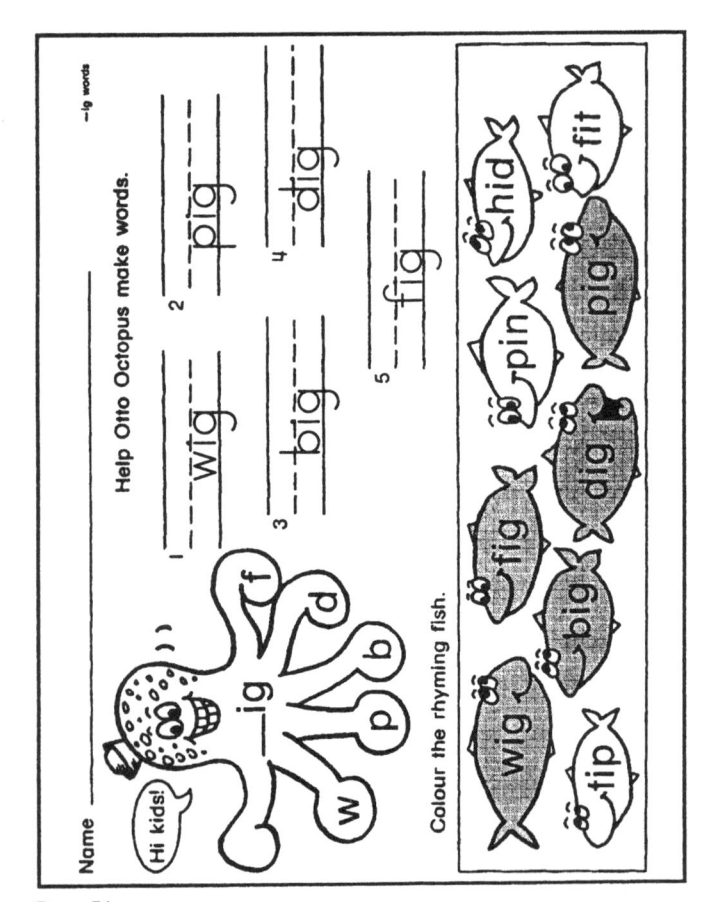

Page 50

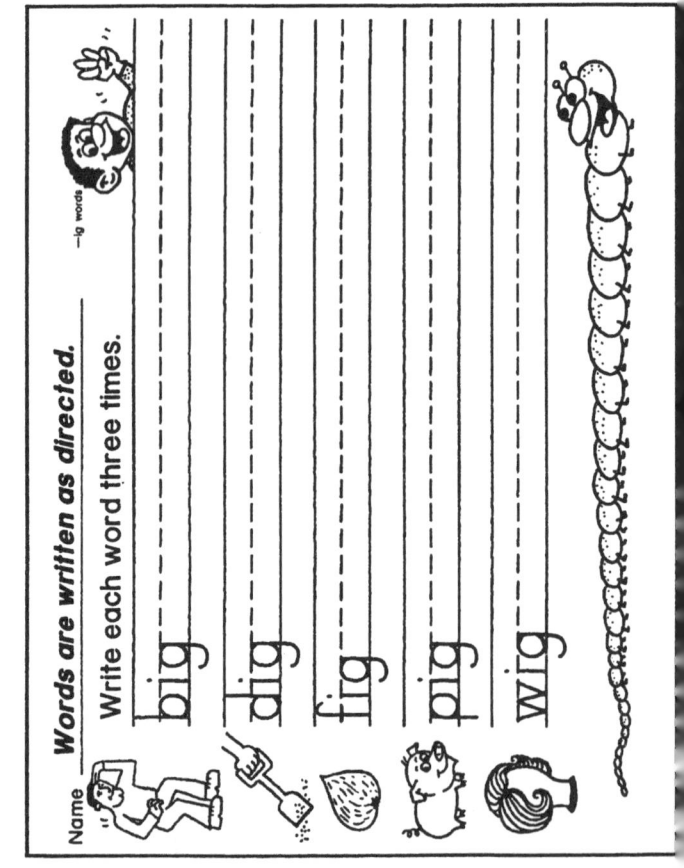

Page 51

Page 52

Answer Key

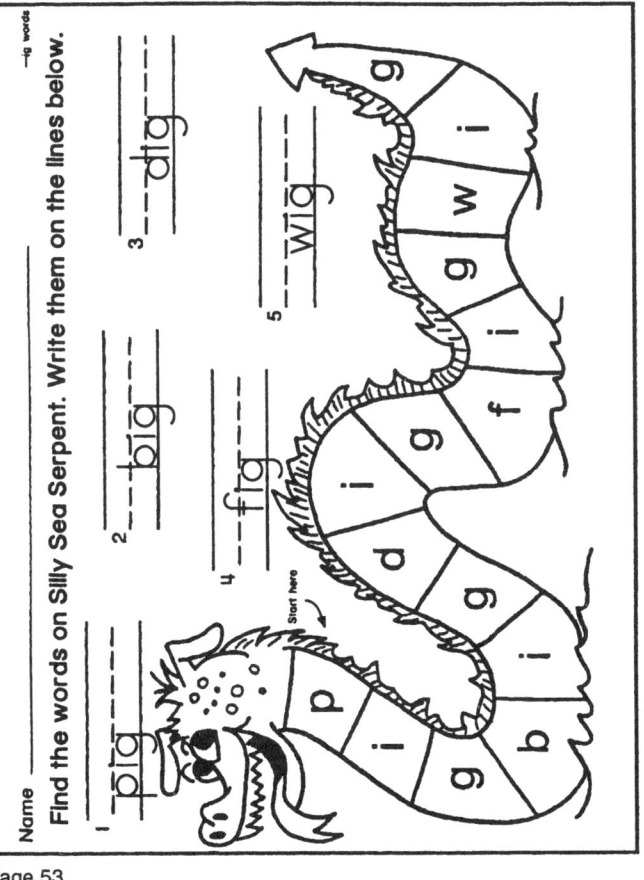

Page 53

Page 54

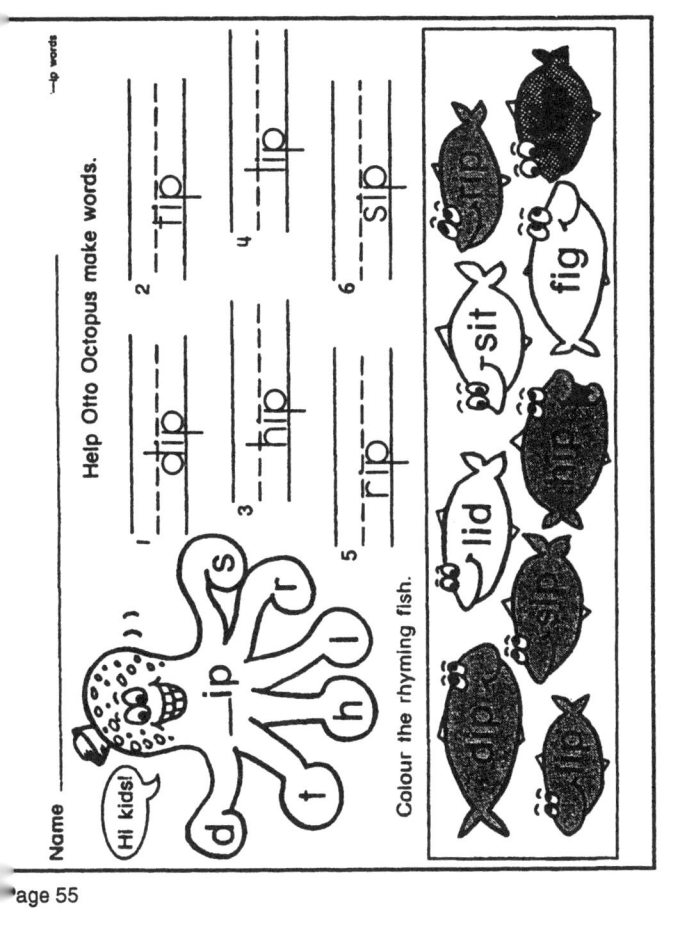

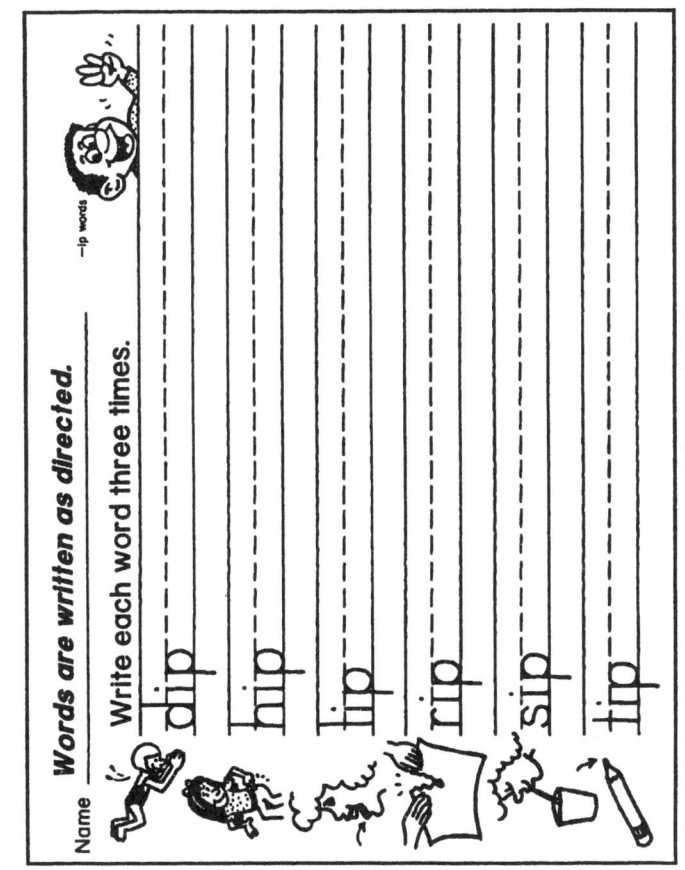

Page 55

Page 56

Answer Key

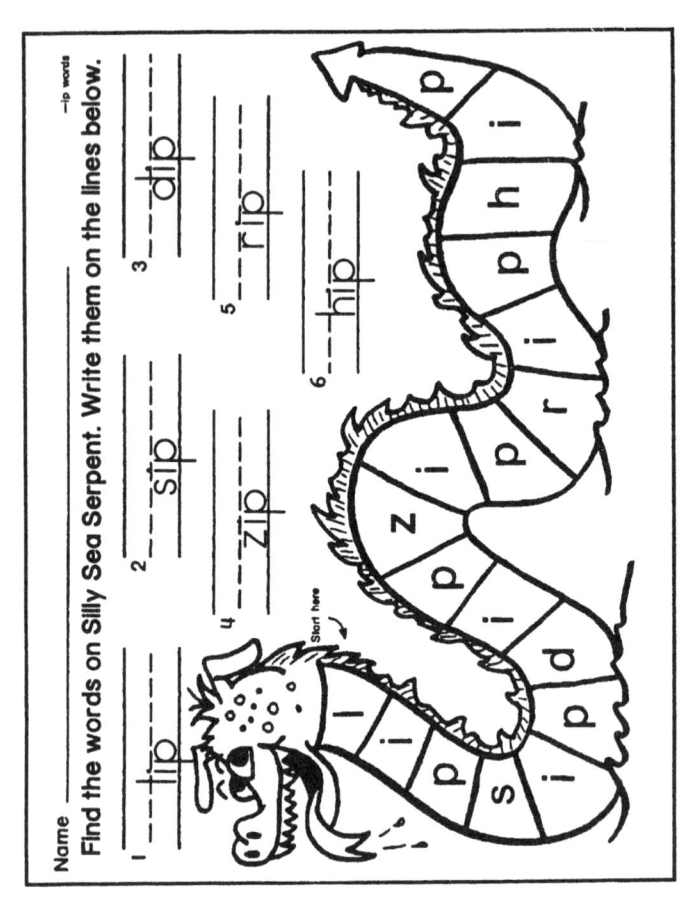

Page 57

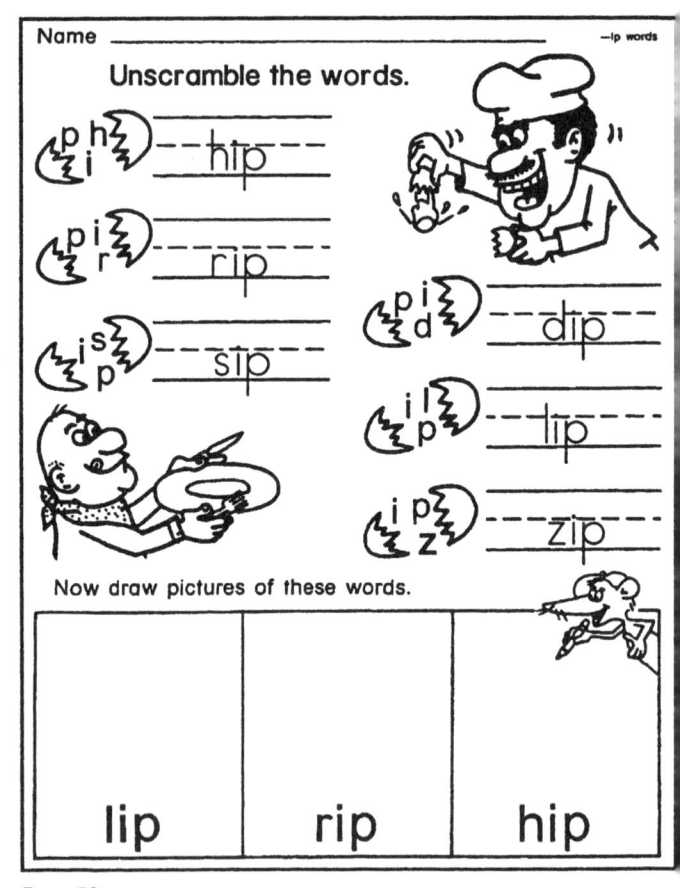

Page 58

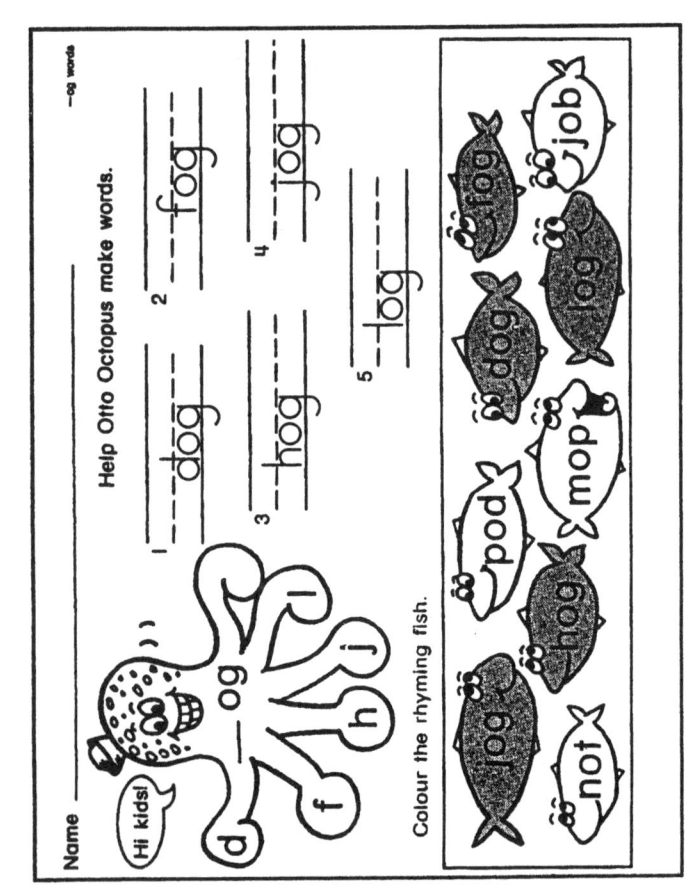

Page 59

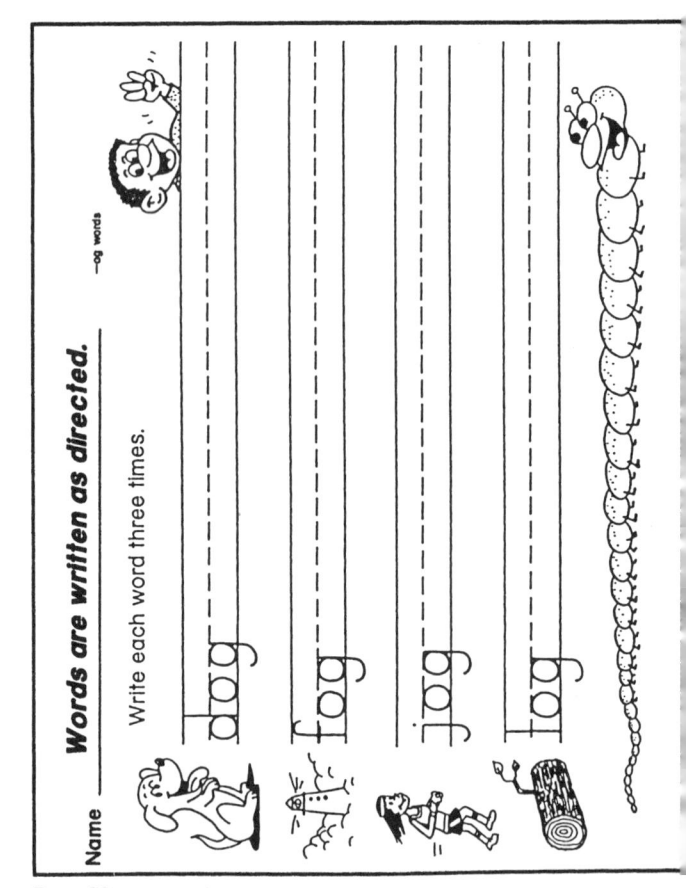

Page 60

113

Answer Key

Page 61

Find the words on Silly Sea Serpent. Write them on the lines below.

1. dog
2. fog
3. hog
4. jog
5. log

Page 62

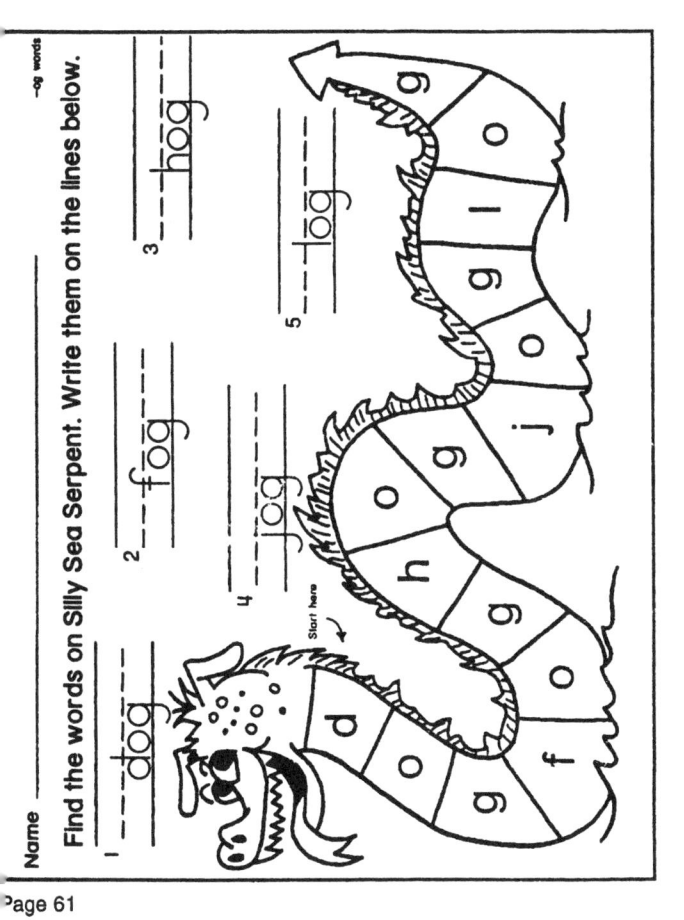

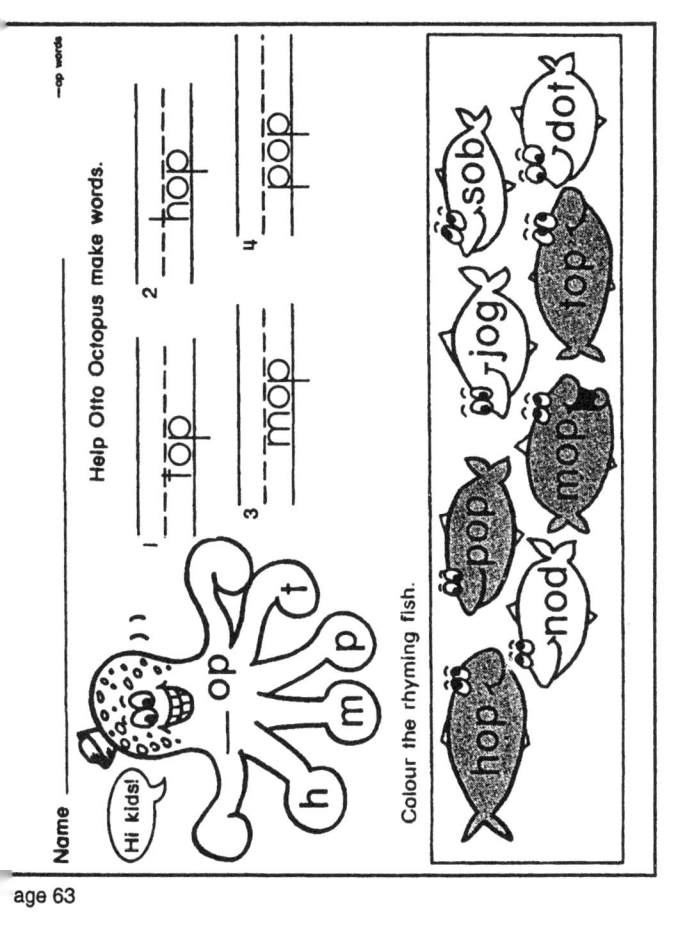

Unscramble the words.

- dog
- fog
- jog
- hog
- log

Now draw pictures of these words.

| dog | jog | log |

Page 63

Help Otto Octopus make words.

1. top
2. hop
3. mop
4. pop

Colour the rhyming fish.

(top, mop, pop, hop)

Page 64

Words are written as directed.

Write each word three times.

- hop
- mop
- pop
- top

114

Copyright © 1996 Brighter Vision Education Ltd   Phonics, KS1

Answer Key

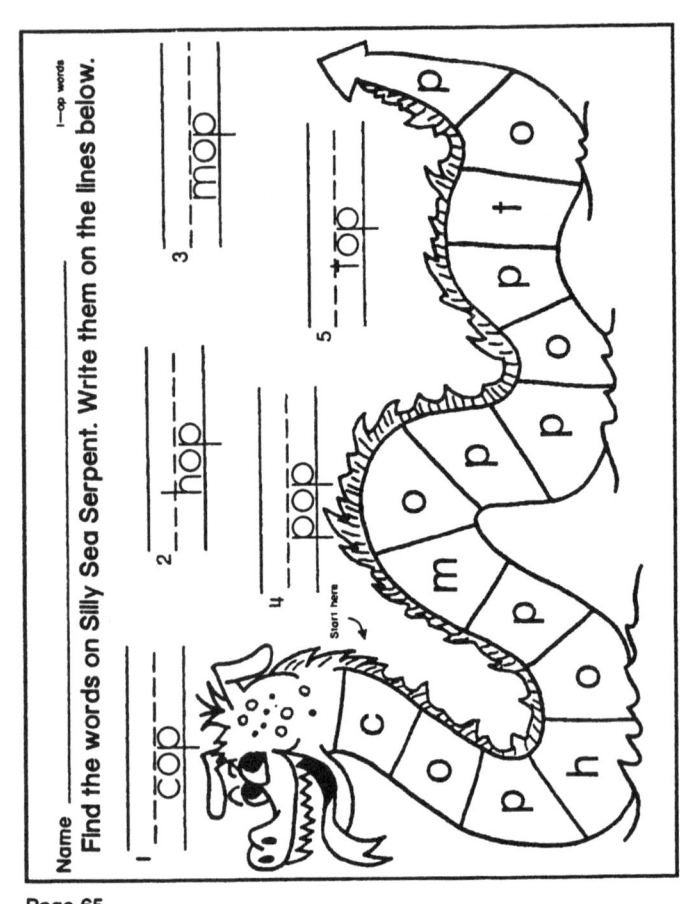

Page 65

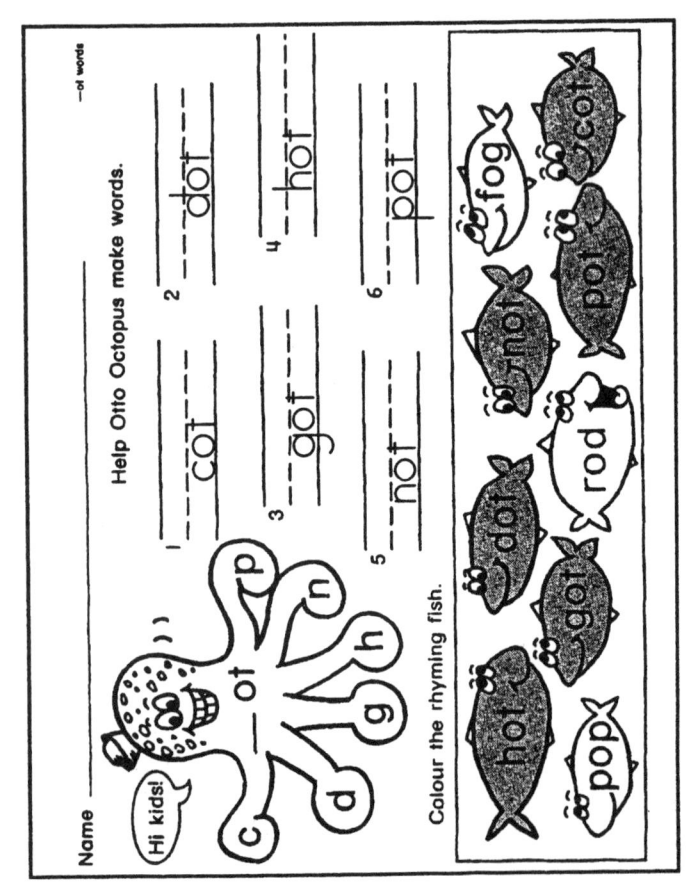

—op words

Find the words on Silly Sea Serpent. Write them on the lines below.

1. cop
2. hop
3. top
4. pop
5. mop

Page 66

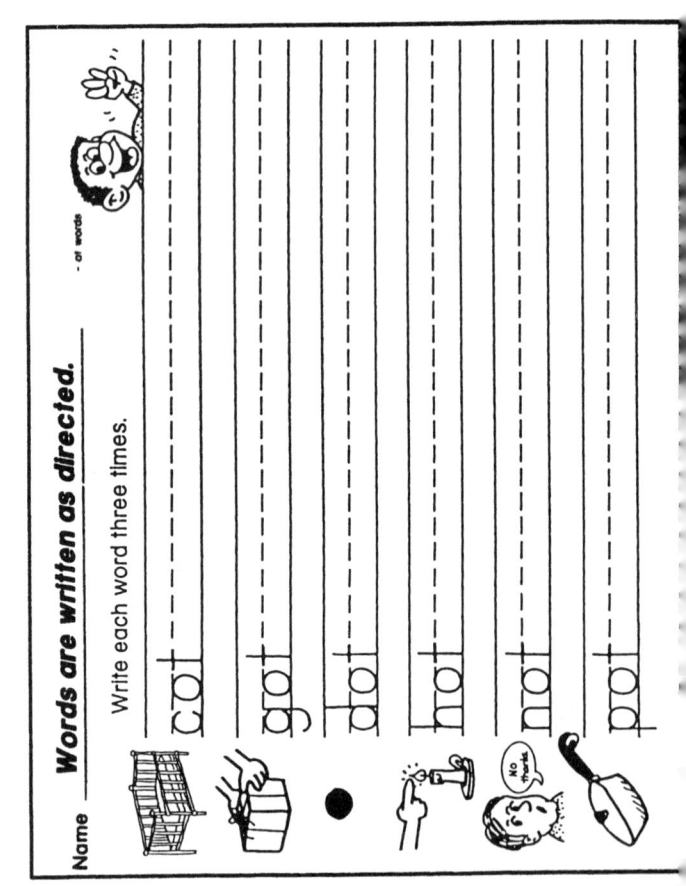

—op words

Unscramble the words.

- hop
- mop
- pop
- top

Now draw pictures of these words.

| top | mop | hop |

Page 67

—ot words

Help Otto Octopus make words.

1. cot
2. dot
3. got
4. hot
5. not
6. pot

Colour the rhyming fish.

(rhyming: cot, pot, not, dot, got, hot; non-rhyming: fog, rod, pop)

Page 68

— ot words

Words are written as directed.

Write each word three times.

cot, got, dot, hot, not, pot

Answer Key

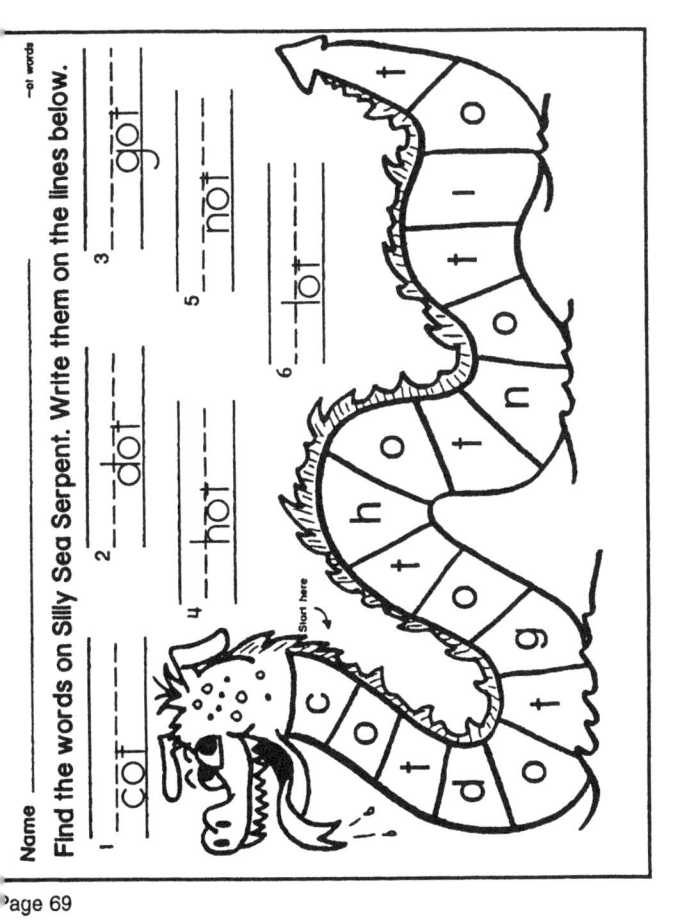

Page 69

Page 70

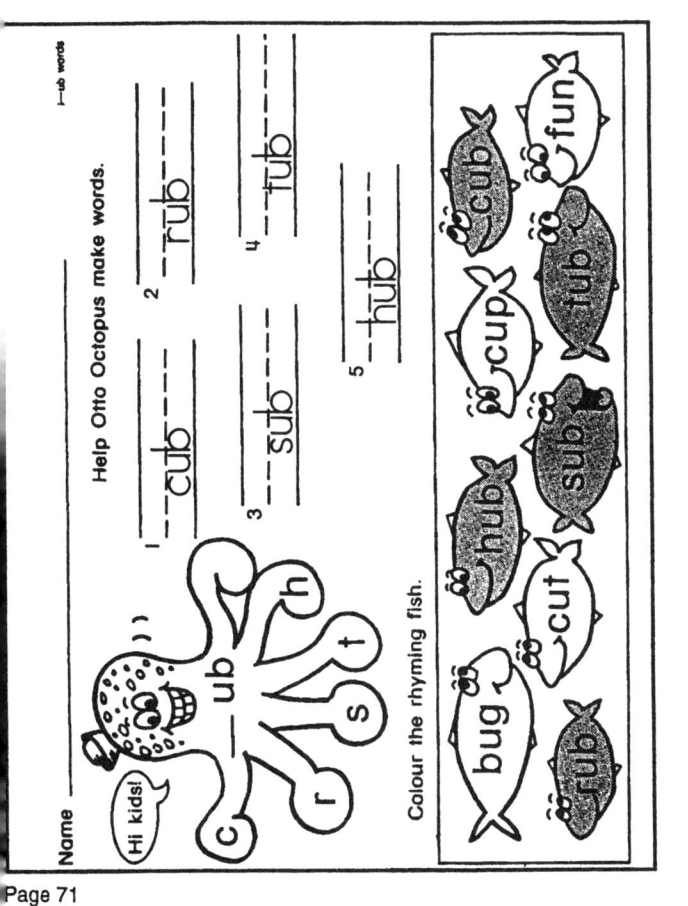

Page 71

Page 72

116

Answer Key

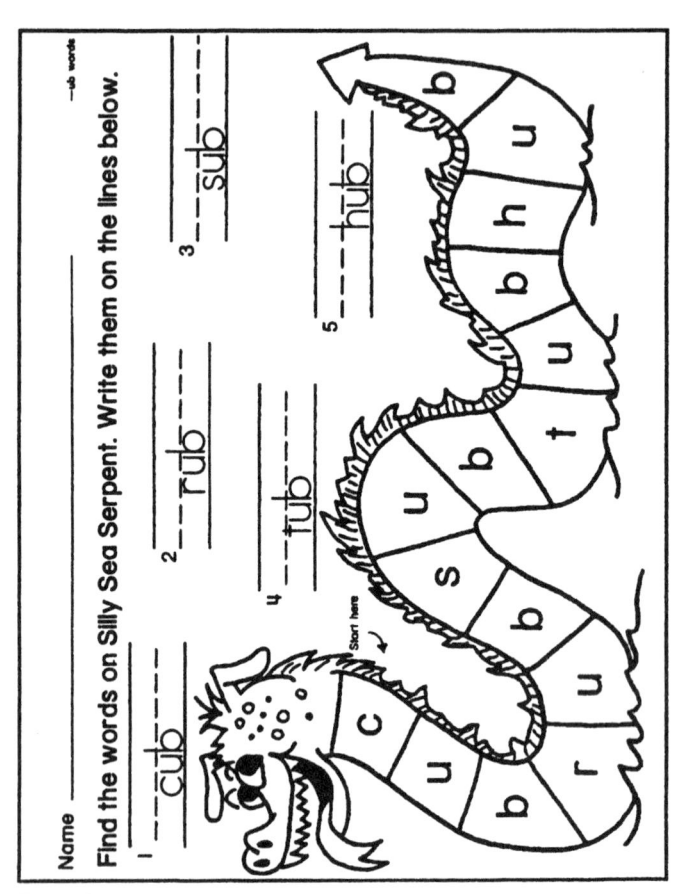

Page 73

Page 74

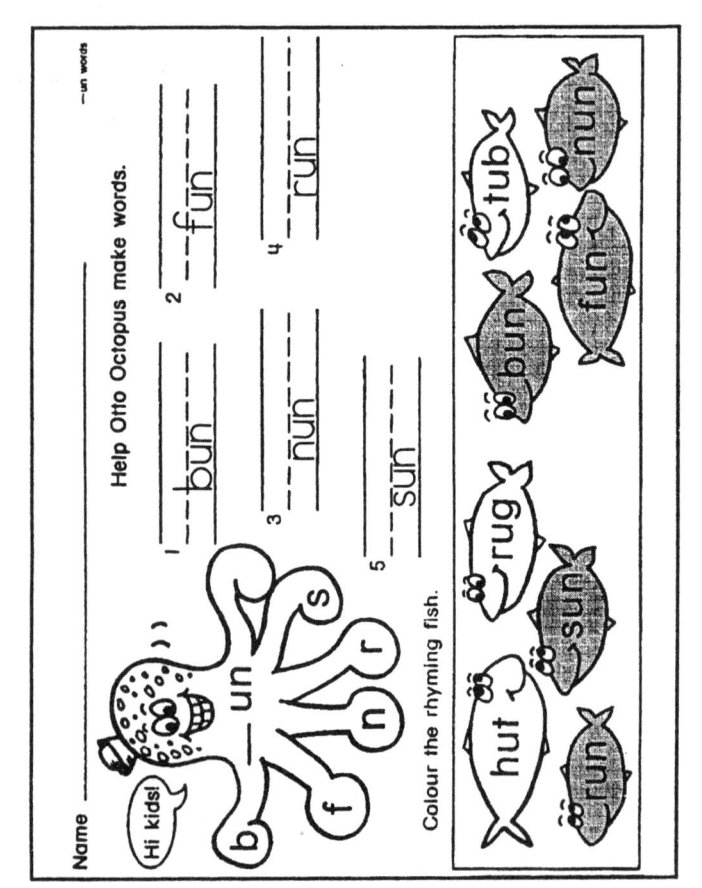

Page 75

Page 76

117

Answer Key

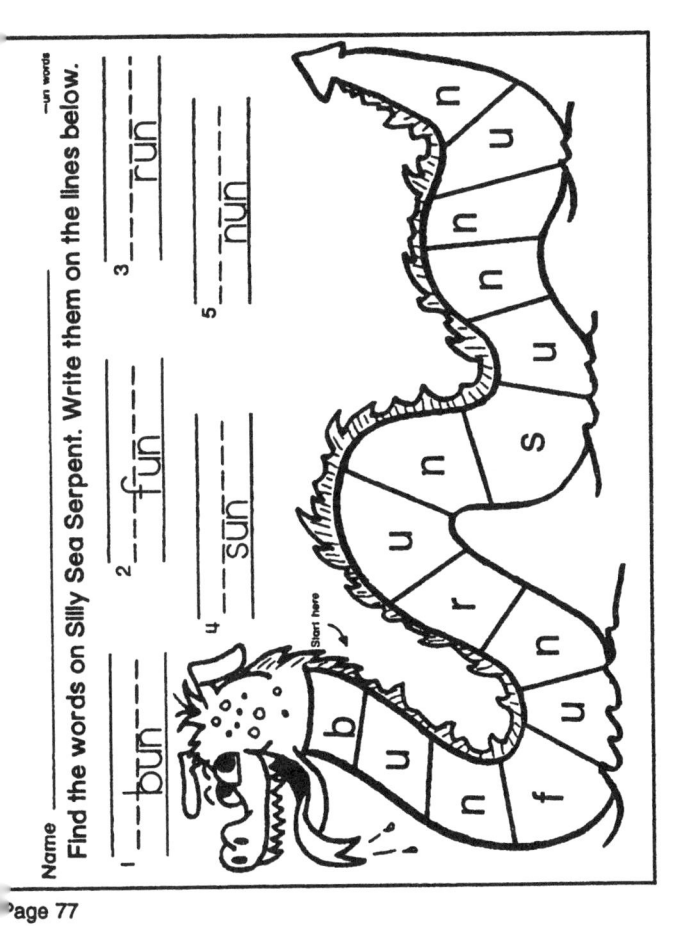

Page 77

Find the words on Silly Sea Serpent. Write them on the lines below.

1. bun
2. fun
3. run
4. sun
5. nun

Page 78

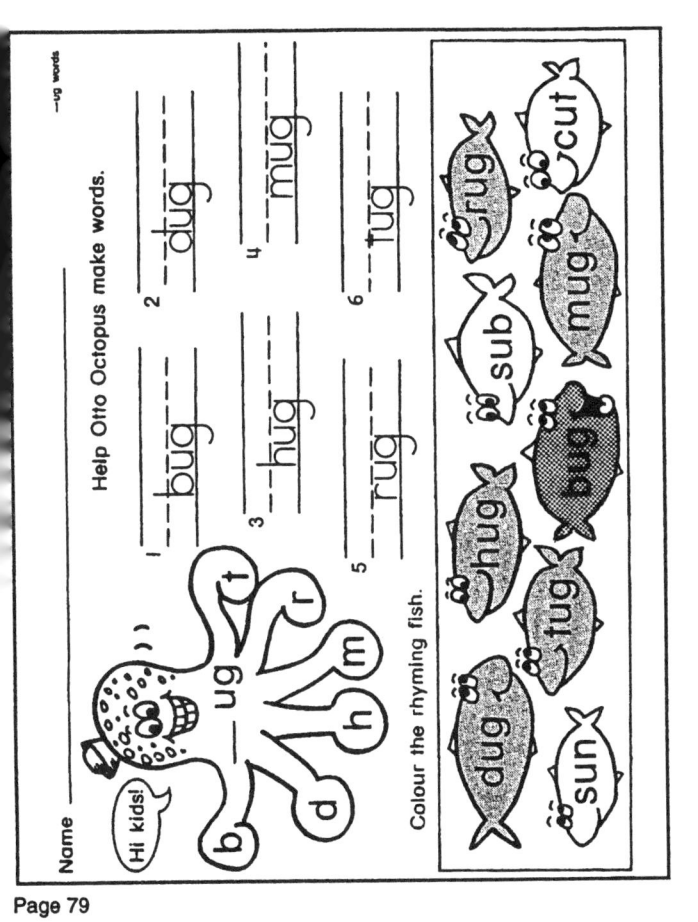

Unscramble the words.

- bun
- fun
- run
- sun
- nun

Now draw pictures of these words: nun, sun, bun

Page 79

Help Otto Octopus make words.

1. bug
2. dug
3. hug
4. mug
5. rug
6. tug

Colour the rhyming fish: rug, mug, hug, bug, tug, dug

Page 80

Words are written as directed. Write each word three times.

bug, hug, mug, rug, tug

Answer Key

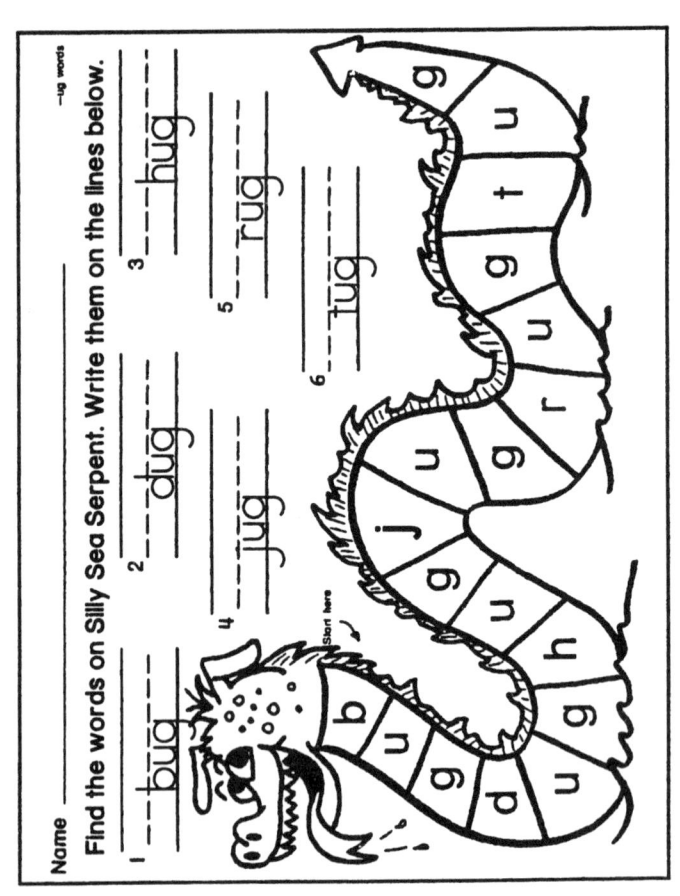

Page 81

Page 82

Page 83

Page 84

119

Copyright © 1996 Brighter Vision Education Ltd

Phonics, KS1

Answer Key

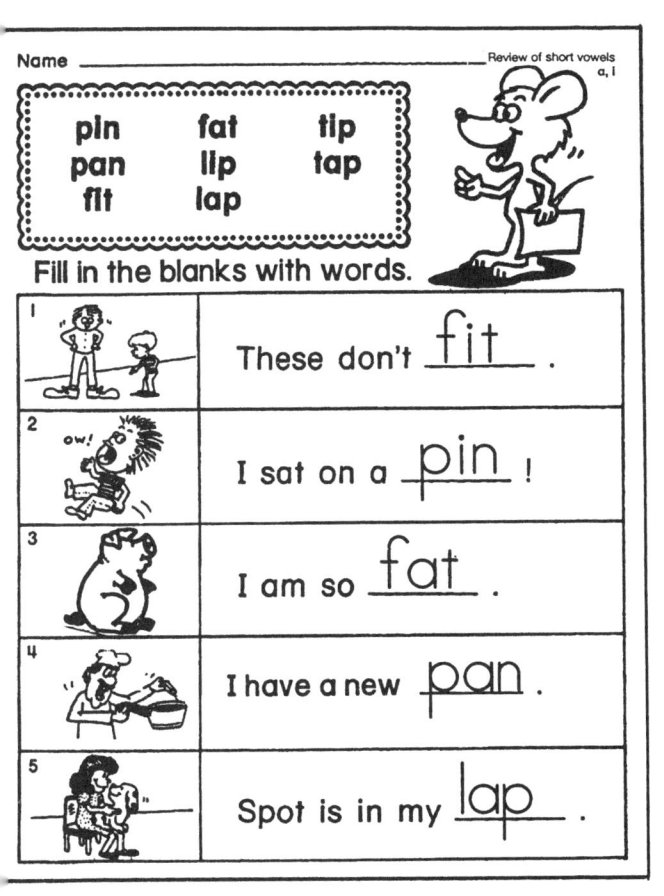

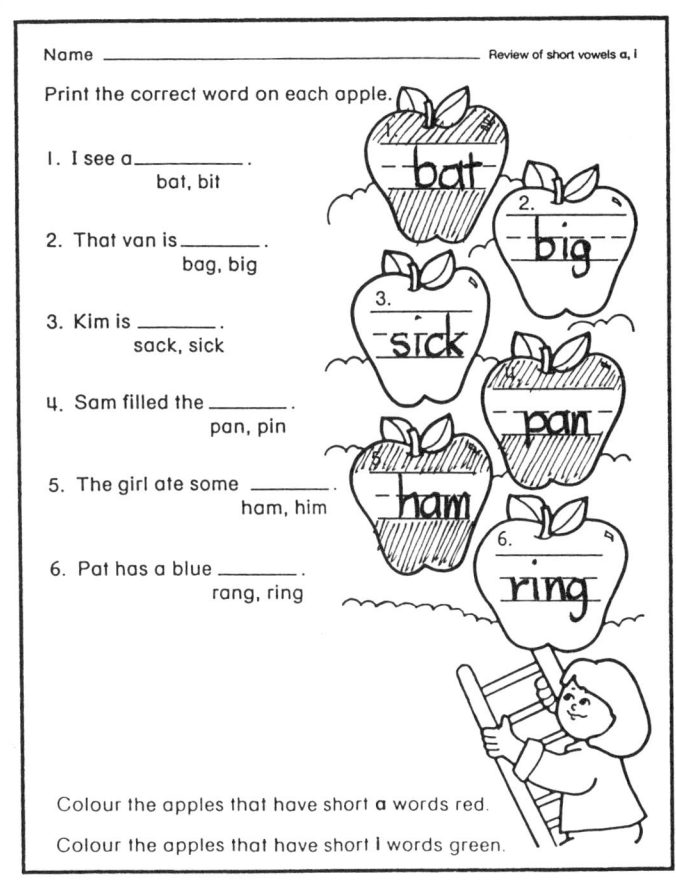

Page 85

Review of short vowels a, i

pin	fat	tip
pan	lip	tap
fit	lap	

Fill in the blanks with words.

1. These don't **fit**.
2. I sat on a **pin**!
3. I am so **fat**.
4. I have a new **pan**.
5. Spot is in my **lap**.

Page 86

Review of short vowels a, i

Print the correct word on each apple.

1. I see a _____. (bat, bit) — **bat**
2. That van is _____. (bag, big) — **big**
3. Kim is _____. (sack, sick) — **sick**
4. Sam filled the _____. (pan, pin) — **pan**
5. The girl ate some _____. (ham, him) — **ham**
6. Pat has a blue _____. (rang, ring) — **ring**

Colour the apples that have short **a** words red.
Colour the apples that have short **i** words green.

Page 87

Review of short vowels i, o

hot	dig	pop
hit	jog	pig
dog	big	

Fill in the blanks with words.

1. You look **big**.
2. I **jog** every day.
3. Pinky is my pet **pig**.
4. Tiny is my pet **dog**.
5. It might **pop**.

Page 88

Review of short vowels a, u

cat	but	hat
cut	fan	hut
bat	fun	

Fill in the blanks with words.

1. I want to, **but** I can't.
2. I have a pet **cat**.
3. That is a **bat**.
4. Ow! I have a **cut**.
5. Turn on the **fan**.

Answer Key

Page 89

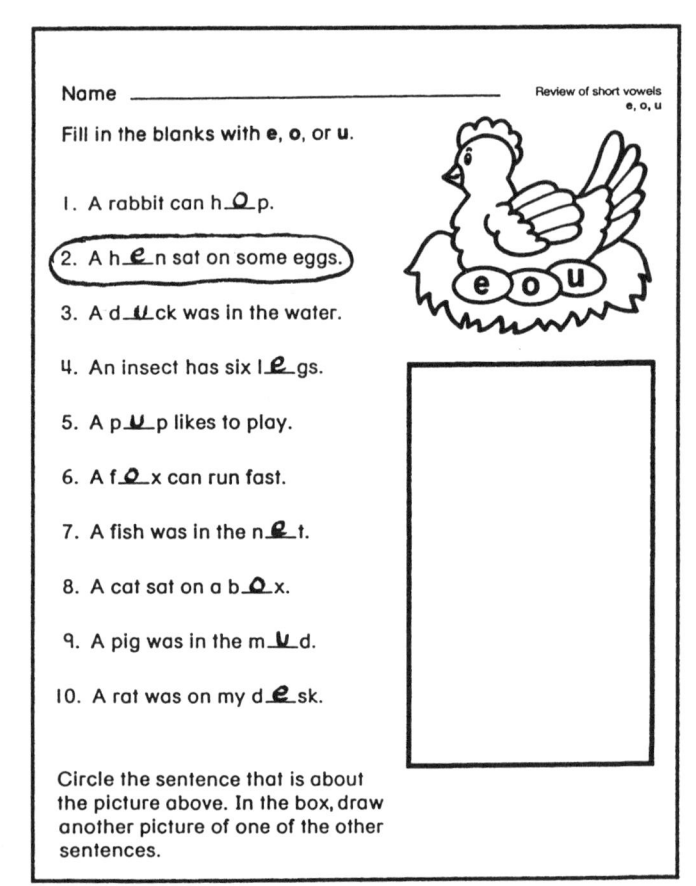

Word box: not, sun, run, hug, dot, hop, top, bug

Fill in the blanks with words.

1. I **run** fast!
2. I am **not** a boy.
3. I love the **sun**.
4. Mum gave me a **hug**.
5. See my new **top**!

Page 90

Print the missing vowel.

p**i**n	d**o**g	h**a**t
p**o**t	r**i**ng	m**o**p
m**a**t	s**o**ck	c**a**n
f**i**sh	t**a**ck	l**o**g

Page 91

Fill in the blanks with **e**, **o**, or **u**.

1. A rabbit can h**o**p.
2. A h**e**n sat on some eggs. *(circled)*
3. A d**u**ck was in the water.
4. An insect has six l**e**gs.
5. A p**u**p likes to play.
6. A f**o**x can run fast.
7. A fish was in the n**e**t.
8. A cat sat on a b**o**x.
9. A pig was in the m**u**d.
10. A rat was on my d**e**sk.

Circle the sentence that is about the picture above. In the box, draw another picture of one of the other sentences.

Page 92

Print the missing vowel.

b**o**x	c**a**p	s**u**n
r**i**ng	d**o**ll	f**a**n
t**o**p	l**o**g	s**i**x
b**a**t	p**i**n	c**u**p

Answer Key

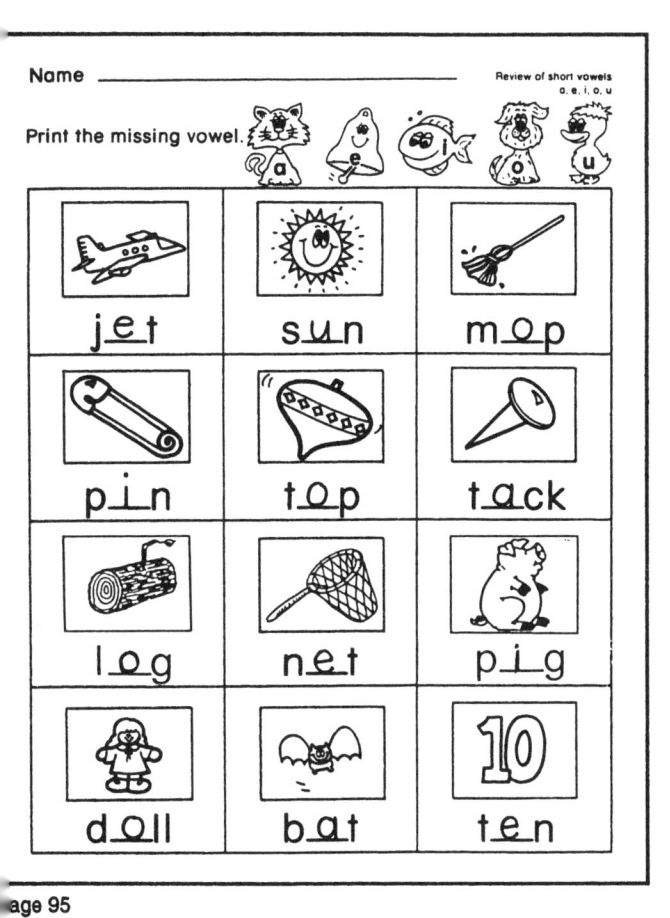

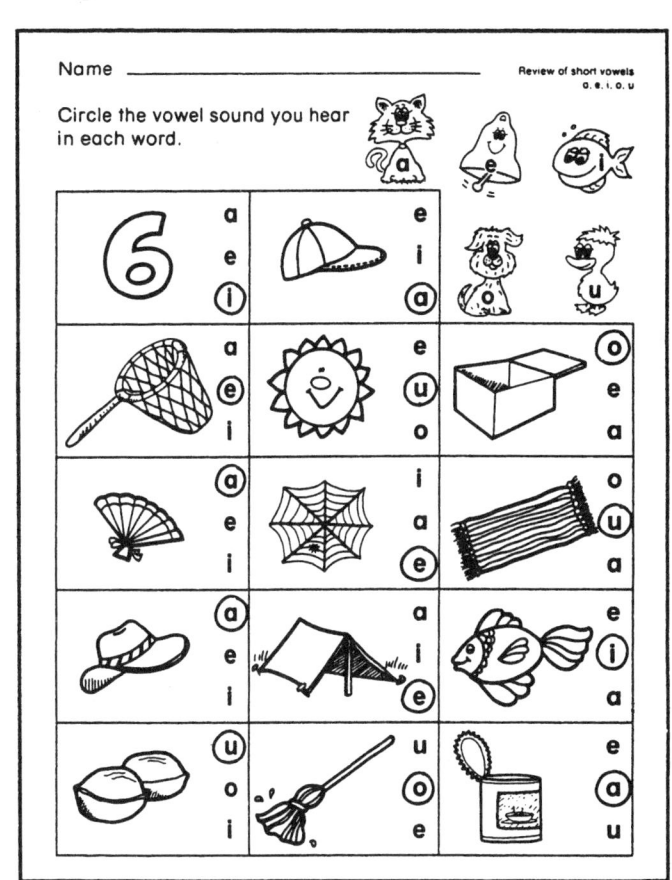

Page 93

Page 94

Page 95

Page 96

122

Answer Key

Page 97

Name _____ Review of short vowels a, e, i, o, u

Circle the word for each picture.

(pin)	pan / pen / **(pin)**	fan	**(fan)** / fin / fun	log	lag / **(log)** / lug
net	**(net)** / not / nut	hut	hat / hit / **(hut)**	pot	pat / pet / **(pot)**
sock	sack / sick / **(sock)**	ten	tan / **(ten)** / tin	lock	lick / **(lock)** / luck
ring	rang / **(ring)** / rung	lamp	**(lamp)** / limp / lump	bell	ball / **(bell)** / bill

Page 98

Name _____ Short vowels a, e, i, o, u

Circle the word for each picture.

hut	hat / hit / **(hut)**	cat	**(cat)** / cot / cut	hat	**(hat)** / hot / hut
duck	deck / dock / **(duck)**	pin	pan / pen / **(pin)**	dog	dig / **(dog)** / dug
ring	rang / **(ring)** / rung	bat	**(bat)** / bet / but	lock	lick / **(lock)** / luck
sock	sack / sick / **(sock)**	lamp	**(lamp)** / limp / lump	bell	ball / **(bell)** / bill